FAMILY CELEBRATIONS AT THANKSGIVING

And Alternatives to Halloween

Ann Hibbard

A Raven's Ridge Book

Baker Books

A Division of Baker Book House Co
Grand Rapids, Michigan 49516

Published by Raven's Ridge Books
an imprint of Baker Book House Company
P.O. Box 6287, Grand Rapids, MI 49516-6287

Second printing, October 1995

Printed in the United States of America

Library of Congress Cataloging-in-Publication Data

Hibbard, Ann, 1956–
    Family celebrations at Thanksgiving and alternatives to Halloween / Ann Hibbard.
       p.   cm.
    "A Raven's Ridge Book."
    Includes bibliographical references.
    ISBN 0-8010-4400-6 (pbk.)
    1. Christian education—Home training. 2. Family—Religious life. 3. Activity programs in Christian education. 4. Holidays—United States. 5. All Saints' Day. 6. All Saints' Day—Prayer-books and devotions—English. 7. Christian saints—Prayer-books and devotions—English. 8. Halloween. 9. Thanksgiving Day. 10. Thanksgiving Day—Prayer-books and devotions—English. I. Title.
BV1590.H47   1995
249—dc20
                                          95–19660

Contents

FAMILY
CELEBRATIONS
AT
THANKSGIVING

A NOTE TO PARENTS

Autumn. Crisp, cool air, skies of vivid blue, trees aflame with color: It is a season of beginnings. (Never mind New Year's—for me the new year will always begin right after Labor Day!) There is a sense of excitement and renewed energy after the dog days of summer. Ready to take on the world, we plunge once more into the school scene. We settle into a new schedule, a new slate of activities.

Then comes October and with it a month-long barrage of Halloween hype. Christians are becoming increasingly uncomfortable with this questionable holiday. Should we swim against the tide of our culture by refusing to participate in a holiday of devilish origins? Or do we decide to pick our battles, taking a stand on more essential matters?

This book does not make that choice for you. I believe that this is an area where personal conviction should dictate.

Rather than jumping into the Halloween fray, I have chosen to focus on a positive alternative—the celebration of All Saints' Day. For centuries Christians have celebrated All Saints' Day on November 1. Let's reclaim this holiday by reintroducing All Saints' Day and celebrating it in our homes. The meaning of this holiday is discussed more fully in the chapter entitled "Wailing Ghosts or Departed Saints?"

I have written family devotions for the ten days preceding All Saints' Day focusing on saints (people who loved God) in church history. I have used the ten-day countdown approach for two years' worth of family devotions. For year one, ten different church fathers and martyrs are examined. During the ten days of year two's devotions, we look at the lives of great missionaries from the past several centuries. This was my first foray into church history—and was it ever inspiring! I came away with a determination to read with my family biographies of the giants of the faith.

Wrap up this season with an All Saints' party on the eve of All Saints' Day (Halloween). This will provide a fun alternative to trick-or-treating for your children. You will find ideas for party games and activities on pages 63–69.

Then comes November. Everyone looks forward to celebrating Thanksgiving on the fourth Thursday of that month. Harness that excitement and channel it into learning together about becoming God's thankful people.

Just as with All Saints' Day, I have written two series of family devotions for the ten days preceding Thanksgiving. During year one, we look at the lives of the prophets Elijah and Elisha. God provided for them and used them to provide for others in many incredible ways. These accounts remind us of all the daily blessings that God provides for us. In year two we look at some of the spiritual blessings that are ours in Christ Jesus—ten of the myriad blessings that his death on the cross provides for those who believe in him.

You will find several suggestions for family activities that reinforce these Thanksgiving devotions and help the family learn about gratitude while having fun together. Finally, there is a brief format for family worship on Thanksgiving Day, found on pages 137–40.

The resource section includes instructions and patterns for several of the family activities, the complete words and music for the hymns used in the devotions, and a list of the books I used while researching the lives of the saints.

I have tried to give you a complete manual for celebrating the seasons of Halloween and Thanksgiving in a new and Christ-centered way. My prayer is that your entire family will grow in faith and commitment to the Lord Jesus Christ during these celebrations.

ALL SAINTS' DAY:
AN ALTERNATIVE
TO
HALLOWEEN

WAILING GHOSTS OR
DEPARTED SAINTS?

T he hammer struck the nail with several determined, well-placed blows. With fire in his eyes and his jaw set, the young priest turned from the cathedral door, leaving the parchment treatise to flutter in the chill October air.

A passerby witnessing this scene scarcely would have given it a second thought. Scholars frequently tacked discourses on the wooden doors of the imposing Castle Church in Wittenburg. Written in Latin, such documents invited other scholars to debate and discussion. Martin Luther's Ninety-Five Theses stated his case against the abuses of the Roman church with the purpose of initiating change within the hierarchy of the church.

When others secretly translated these articles into German and distributed them among the people, the sound of the hammer on the door of Castle Church echoed across all of Germany. Luther himself could not have dreamed that the blows struck that Eve of All Saints, 1517, would still resound five centuries later.

A Historical Perspective

Martin Luther did not choose that day to tack his theses on the door because it was All Hallows' Eve or because the next day was All Saints' Day. Rather, it was the anniversary of the building of the cathedral in Wittenburg. Many people had come to take part in the special services to commemorate this day. Yet because of Martin Luther, a new significance attached itself to this day: October 31 became known as Reformation Day. It marks one of the most important turning points in Christian history.

When October 31 rolls around, however, most of us do not think of Reformation Day. We think of Halloween. The name is derived from All Hallows' (All Saints') Eve. Children love the ritual of dressing in costume and marching from door to door collecting goodies. "Trick or treat!" they cry, their words somewhat muffled by the often grotesque masks covering their faces. All year long, they plan what they will dress up as next Halloween.

Some schools spend the better part of October emphasizing Halloween themes—witches, ghosts, jack-o-lanterns, and black cats are the subjects of stories and crafts. The reason for this seems apparent. Fearful of civil liberties lawsuits, public schools avoid "religious" holidays altogether. The absence of Christmas and Easter creates a huge void, which teachers seek to fill with secular holidays and themes. Halloween is perceived as religiously neutral, and witches and ghosts are seen as imaginary creatures that children enjoy. It is all merely fun—perfectly innocent.

Or is it? On this particular night of the year, vandalism runs rampant. Incidents of razor blades and drugs found in children's treats have been so frequent that many hospitals offer free X rays of Halloween candy. Occasionally the morning papers run a news story describing a suspected human sacrifice performed by Satan worshipers. No one stops to ask the question, Why do so many horrible things happen on Halloween?

Perhaps the answer lies in the origin of the holiday. Halloween as we know it finds its roots in the pagan cultic rites of the ancient Celtic people. The Vikings were a Celtic people, as were the ancient inhabitants of Ireland, Scotland, Wales, and Germany. Their high priests, called druids, taught the worship of things in creation: earth, sky, fire, trees, animals, and the like. These people lived in fear of evil spirits, attributing to them the bad things in their lives. They reasoned that keeping the evil spirits happy was a way of preventing unpleasant circumstances.

One of the Celtic deities was Samhain, the Lord of the Dead, to whom they paid tribute on October 31, the eve of their new year. The druids taught that on this night, the souls of the wicked dead inhabited the bodies of living people in order to be entertained. These possessed people would go out in the countryside to the farmhouses and offer the ultimatum of trick or treat. If the frightened country folk did not provide suitable food, shelter, and entertainment, the trick-or-treaters would destroy the country folks' property and cast evil spells upon their home. In Wales, ghastly faces were carved in gourds, then the gourds were lighted and carried by the trick-or-treaters to aid in spooking the country people.

So, at its foundation, Halloween is a fiendish celebration of death, a tribute to the wicked spirits of the underworld. It was not widely observed in our country until the late 1800s, when a large number of Celtic people immigrated from Europe—people who had never relinquished this yearly observance.

But what is All Saints' Day, and why does it coincide with this pagan festival? All Saints' Day, originally observed in May, was a Christian celebration honoring those who had died in Christ. It was not a day for worshiping the saints, but for remembering them and thanking God for the lives of faith that they led. The date was moved from May to November 1 when on that date Pope Gregory III dedicated a chapel in the basilica of St. Peter to "all the saints." It was Pope Gregory IV who ordered that all Christians observe All Saints' Day on November 1.

All Saints' Day, in and of itself, is a good and worthy celebration, if it is observed in a biblical manner. Based on Hebrews 12:1 and 1 Peter 5:4, the Anglican *Book of Common Prayer* states in its Preface of All Saints' Day:

> For in the multitude of your saints, you have surrounded us with a great cloud of witnesses, that we might rejoice in their fellowship, and run with endurance the race that is set before us; and, together with them, receive the crown of glory that never fades away.

We do not pray to the saints, but we merely take this occasion to remember them and to thank God for the sacrifices they made in order that we might know Jesus Christ.

It can only enrich our faith to acknowledge Martin Luther, John Calvin, and John Knox—giants of the Reformation. At great personal cost, the Wesleys preached throughout England and the colonies the good news of salvation by faith in Jesus Christ.

More recently, saints such as Hudson Taylor, Amy Carmichael, and Jim Elliot poured out their lives for Jesus in remote corners of the world. This is an appropriate occasion to recall those who directly influenced our lives for Christ—parents, youth leaders, that special Christian friend.

All Saints' is a time of thanksgiving to God for those who have gone before us, for those who have been faithful unto death. Instead of celebrating death, let us celebrate life by remembering heroes of the faith.

ALL SAINTS' DAY: AN ALTERNATIVE TO HALLOWEEN

OCTOBER FAMILY ACTIVITIES

Ghosts, goblins, witches, and evil creatures of every sort haunt the aisles of drugstores and the windows of elementary schools during the month of October. Rather than simply reacting negatively to these things, Christian families can be a wonderful witness by doing something positive instead. Here are several suggestions for family activities during October that can make a good difference in our homes and ultimately in our society.

Family Reading: Stories of Great Christians

From the early church to contemporary times, men and women of great faith and commitment have given their lives for the gospel. Their stories inspire us to, in the words of William Carey (see p. 42), "expect great things of God; attempt great things for God."

We learn from those who have gone before us. We see the mistakes that they made and the consequences that followed. Their mistakes warn us against making the same mistakes. We see the great faith that they had and the commitment that led them to forsake the comforts and pleasures of this life in order to reach others for Christ. Their commitment challenges us to make a deeper commitment to Christ.

You and your children will greatly benefit from reading these stories. Peruse your church library or Christian bookstore for several good biographies that might hold your children's interest during family reading. I have given brief sketches of selected saints for each day of the family devotions. One of these stories might whet your appetite to learn more about that particular figure.

The resource I found most helpful was Ruth Tucker's wonderful volume, *From Jerusalem to Irian Jaya: A Biographical History of Christian Missions*. This book records the highlights from the lives of about one hundred missionaries spanning the years from the time of the apostle Paul to today.

The Tree of Saints

The Tree of Saints is simply a bare tree branch from your yard or park that is placed in a vase and hung with pictures of God's great men and women of faith. Each of the family devotions for All Saints' has a corresponding symbol—a round circle with a drawing depicting the saint studied that day.

Two to three weeks before All Saints', spend a fun family evening constructing the symbols. Patterns and instructions can be found in the resource section at the back of the book. Construct the symbols ahead of time so you will be ready to hang each day's symbol on the Tree of Saints during the ten countdown days. There is a special time to hang the symbol on the tree at the conclusion of each day's devotional.

Not only is this a fun activity that involves the entire family, but it also reinforces what you have read. It is a visual reminder of the character. When the children see the symbol, they remember the story and how that saint's life is an example to us.

All Saints' Goody Bag

If we don't want our children to go trick-or-treating, it seems like a good idea to provide another way for our children to have goodies. We don't want them to feel like they are being punished for being Christians. (I confess, I would never want to be deprived of chocolate!)

Two weeks before All Saints', have your children each decorate a goody bag. Use a heroes of the faith theme: They can draw and color their favorite Bible heroes on the bag. Glitter glue (messy but fun), yarn, fabric, cotton balls, and other extras can help to make this an exciting, creative time for your children.

Have on hand several bags of your children's favorite candies or goodies. Then each evening after your family devotions, each child gets to put a goody in his or her bag. The goodies keep accumulating until All Saints' Day, when they can begin to eat them.

Explain to the children that each goody reminds us that each of these men and women of faith lived their lives for God, and a life lived for God is sweet to God. The goodies also remind us of all the good things we have because others gave their lives to bring us God's Word.

All Saints' Party

For a positive alternative to trick-or-treating or Halloween parties on October 31, see the chapter entitled "All Saints' Party."

All Saints' Family Worship

Here are prayers, responsive readings, hymn singing, and suggestions for meaningful family worship on All Saints' Day.

ALL SAINTS' DEVOTIONS: YEAR ONE

OCTOBER 22

DAY 10

Polycarp was a leader of the church after the apostles died. He was born in A.D. 70 and died at the age of eighty-six, in A.D. 156. Polycarp was a student of John, Jesus' "beloved disciple." He lived in Smyrna (what is now Turkey).

Being a Christian was a very dangerous thing in those days. Many Christians were tortured and killed because they did not worship the pagan gods that everyone else worshiped. During this difficult time, Polycarp was a strong and loving leader to the Christians in his care. He wrote a letter to the church at Philippi (the same church that Paul wrote to in the book of Philippians) that records his commitment to the truth of the gospel as well as his concern for fellow believers.

One day a bloodthirsty crowd was celebrating a pagan holiday by conducting gruesome games in the amphitheater—a huge outdoor arena. The crowd had already killed one young man and chose Polycarp to be the next object of their "fun."

A group found Polycarp at a nearby farm. He invited them to eat a meal while he spent an hour in prayer. After the hour, they questioned and made fun of him, trying to get him to say that he did not believe in Jesus. Polycarp answered them, "For eighty-six years I have been his servant and he has never done me wrong. How can I blaspheme my king who saved me?"

When the mob at the amphitheater received news of what Polycarp said, they were furious and first called for him to be thrown to the lions, then shouted for him to be burned at the stake. An official tied Polycarp's hands and feet and ran him through with a sword, then burned his body.

Discuss

1. Has anyone ever made fun of you because you were a Christian or because you did what was right?
2. How did you feel? What did you do?

3. From this account, what do we learn about the kind of person Polycarp was? How would you describe him?
4. How can Polycarp's example help you in the situations you face at school, at work, or in the neighborhood?

Final Thought

The other day my son came home from school looking pale and shaken. He told me that as the bus drove up our street, a neighbor boy who hates him (for no reason, it seems) picked up a rock and threw it at his window. We need to be ready for persecution, and just as Polycarp did, we must meet our enemies with an unshakable faith and the love of Jesus Christ.

Pray

Dear Lord Jesus Christ, help me to grow strong in my faith so that when troubles come, I stand firm, trusting you. Amen.

Sing—*My Faith Looks Up to Thee* (p. 174)

May thy rich grace impart
Strength to my fainting heart,
My zeal inspire;
As thou hast died for me,
Oh, may my love to thee
Pure, warm, and changeless be,
A living fire!

Do

Place the symbol of Polycarp on your Tree of Saints.

Further Study for Adults

Read 1 Peter 4:12–19. What two kinds of suffering does Peter mention here? What should be our attitude toward suffering as a Christian? Why? Is there a situation in your life right now to which these principles apply? What steps can you take today to begin to respond as these verses command?

OCTOBER 23

DAY 9

Perpetua was a young widow with an infant son. She lived in Carthage, a city in North Africa, at the turn of the third century. She and several other companions became Christians at a time when the Roman emperor decreed that everyone must worship him as a god and sacrifice to him. The punishment for refusing to do this was death.

Of course, Perpetua and her friends would not worship the emperor. Government officials arrested and imprisoned these young believers. While in prison, Perpetua had many visions. In one vision, Perpetua climbed a ladder and reached a large garden she interpreted to mean heaven. In another vision, she saw her brother who had died of a disease many years before. In this vision, he was well and was drinking the water of life. Her final vision was of a battle with the devil, in which she was a young warrior who overthrew the devil in unarmed single combat. After this vision, she wrote, "And I awoke, understanding that I should fight, not with beasts, but with the devil."

After many days in prison Perpetua was brought to trial. At the trial, even her elderly father begged her to worship the emperor. She refused, saying, "I am a Christian." She and her companions were sent to the arena to be mauled by wild animals in front of cheering crowds. In the midst of the attack, Perpetua encouraged her fellow martyrs, saying, "Stand fast in the faith and love one another. And do not let what we suffer be a stumbling block to you." Injured but not killed by the animals, Perpetua and her friends were eventually put to death by the sword. The soldier who tried to kill Perpetua missed, merely injuring her further. Perpetua helped him guide the sword in the stroke that killed her.

Discuss

1. Why did Perpetua refuse to worship the emperor?
2. What did she say when she and her friends were being attacked by wild animals in the arena? What do her words mean?

3. What new understanding did Perpetua have after her vision of her battle with the devil?

4. What do you most admire about Perpetua? How can you be more like her?

Final Thought

What a strong faith Perpetua had, even though she was a new Christian! She loved the Lord so much that she was willing to brave a horrible death, leaving behind an infant son and a disappointed father. I wonder if I would leave my children motherless because I refused to worship someone other than Jesus? How about you?

Pray

Lord Jesus Christ, you are the giver of faith and courage. Enable us to stand up for you today. Amen.

Sing—*O Jesus, I Have Promised* (p. 176)

O Jesus, I have promised
To serve you to the end;
Remain forever near me,
My master and my friend.
I shall not fear the battle
If you are by my side,
Nor wander from the pathway
If you will be my guide.

Do

Place the symbol of Perpetua on your Tree of Saints.

Further Study for Adults

Read 1 Peter 5:8–11. How does Peter depict Satan in these verses? How are we to overcome the evil one? What encouragement does God give us in this passage? How will we be made strong? What difference will these truths make in your life today?

OCTOBER 24

DAY 8

Athanasius was a leader of the early church who, throughout his entire life, fought for truth. God used this courageous man to keep the church from veering off the path of truth and accepting teachings about Jesus that would have destroyed the church.

Athanasius was born in A.D. 295 in Alexandria, Egypt. He became a deacon in his twenties. He then became the assistant to Alexander, the bishop of Alexandria.

At this time a leader named Arius began teaching that Jesus was not fully God. Athanasius spoke out against this teaching. The teachings of Arius caused so many problems that leaders of the church from around the world gathered at Nicaea (in North Africa) in 325 to discuss the matter. This group wrote the great statement of faith known as the Nicene Creed. Athanasius was the one who made sure that this statement clearly expressed that Jesus is fully God. Athanasius penned the words "of one Being with the Father."

Athanasius became bishop in 328, when Alexander died. He wrote many books, papers, sermons, and letters. In all of his writing and speaking, he boldly taught the truth about Jesus Christ and salvation through faith in him.

Many powerful people fought against him: leaders in the church, in government, even the Roman emperor himself. Five times he was sent into exile. Yet the people of Alexandria grew to love him. The last time Athanasius was exiled, the people were so enraged that the emperor decided to call him back to the city before rioting erupted.

Because of his uncompromising stand for truth, Athanasius has been called "the pillar of the church" and "the God-given physician of her wounds." He died in 373.

Discuss

1. What made Athanasius an important leader?
2. What was Athanasius called? Why?

3. Why is it important to believe that Jesus is fully God?
4. Think of a time when you have had to stand up for the truth about Jesus. What happened?

Final Thought

What would the world be like today if Athanasius had not insisted that Jesus is fully God? The meaning of the cross and Jesus' death for our salvation would have been lost. You and I would not be Christians today. Most of the good of our society comes from the influence of the church, people whose lives have been changed by the living Christ.

Pray

Dear Lord Christ, you are God in human flesh. Thank you for leaders like Athanasius, who fought for the truth. Thank you for the difference that this truth has made in my life and in the world. Amen.

Sing—*O Word of God Incarnate* (p. 177)

O Word of God incarnate,
O Wisdom from on high,
O Truth unchanged, unchanging,
O Light of our dark sky:
We praise you for the radiance
That from the hallowed page,
A lantern to our footsteps,
Shines on from age to age.

Do

Place the symbol of Athanasius on your Tree of Saints.

Further Study for Adults

Read John 1:1–5, 14 and Colossians 1:15–20. How might these have been key passages for Athanasius? What do we learn about the incarnation in these verses? List the truths about Jesus found here; then write the difference each of these truths makes to you.

OCTOBER 25

DAY 7

Ambrose was the first Latin church father to be raised and educated as a Christian. He came from a leading political family in Rome, and he was the first from this family to take a stand publicly for the church.

He was born in A.D. 339 and at the age of thirty was appointed governor of upper Italy. In the midst of a terrible argument between the Arians (those who didn't think Jesus was fully God) and the orthodox Christians, Ambrose stepped in to make peace. The quarreling crowd called for Ambrose to become the new bishop. Ambrose resisted but finally agreed. As bishop, Ambrose became a great peacemaker, hymn writer, preacher, and pastor.

Ambrose worked hard to free the church from the rule of the Roman government. When the court wanted to take over several churches in Milan, Ambrose organized a peaceful resistance. He spoke time and again of his readiness to suffer and die for Christ, saying, "I know that whatever I must suffer, I shall suffer for Christ's sake." This approach was successful, and the government eventually gave up its fight against Ambrose when even the soldiers left their posts and joined the faithful Christians.

Preaching was Ambrose's greatest gift and calling. He preached powerfully about baptism, the Trinity, and the person of Christ. His preaching played an important role in the conversion of Augustine of Hippo. Ambrose is perhaps best known for his hymns honoring Christ. Several of these hymns are still sung in Christian churches around the world today, including "Savior of the Nations, Come!" Ambrose died of an illness on April 4, 397, with his arms extended to form a cross.

Discuss

1. What were some of the gifts that Ambrose possessed?
2. How did Ambrose use these gifts in Christ's service?
3. What are some of the special gifts that God has given you?
4. How might you use them to serve him?

Final Thought

Ambrose wrote these words: "Lord Jesus Christ, you are for me medicine when I am sick; you are my strength when I need help; you are life itself when I fear death; you are the way when I long for heaven; you are light when all is dark; you are my food when I need nourishment." Ambrose was a man of intelligence, position, and great ability. He used all these gifts in serving Christ. And he depended on Christ to supply all his needs.

Pray

Lord Jesus Christ, may I say with Ambrose that you are my medicine, strength, life, way, light, and food. All that I need I find in you alone. Amen.

Sing—*O Word of God Incarnate* (p. 177)

The Church from you, dear Master,
Received the gift divine;
And still that light is lifted
O'er all the earth to shine.
It is the chart and compass
That, all life's voyage through,
Mid mists and rocks and quicksands
Still guides, O Christ, to you.

Do

Place the symbol of Ambrose on your Tree of Saints.

Further Study for Adults

Read Colossians 1:9–14. What requests does Paul make in this prayer on behalf of the Colossian Christians? What has God already done? What is he in the process of doing? What is the end that God (and Paul) has in mind? Write this prayer in your own words and use it to pray for loved ones, as well as yourself.

OCTOBER 26

DAY 6

John Chrysostom was one of the most beloved fathers of the Eastern church. Born in Antioch, he lived from A.D. 347 to 407. Chrysostom was not a good-looking man, nor was he healthy. But he had a great gift for preaching the gospel, and this is what he loved to do above all else. He said, "Preaching makes me healthy; as soon as I open my mouth, all tiredness is gone." Through his simple but powerful sermons, Chrysostom influenced many people in his day as well as succeeding generations. Chrysostom said, "I cannot let a day pass without feeding you with the treasures of the Scriptures."

During his life he was known as John. Years after his death, he was given the name Chrysostom, which means "golden-tongued," because of his effective preaching. He was not fancy or fiery in his manner; he spoke the truth in such a way that everyone could understand it.

In the year 397, Chrysostom was virtually kidnapped, brought to the church of Constantinople, and appointed bishop of that region, against his will. Usually the bishop of that great city gave lovely parties and socialized with all the important people. Not Chrysostom. He had a heart for the poor and downtrodden, and he spent much time and money helping the needy. He preached against the pleasure-seeking and luxury of the upper classes. He lived very simply.

This kind of preaching and lifestyle produced powerful enemies. His enemies accused him of all sorts of things and succeeded in getting him banished twice. He died on a forced march during his second exile, with the words "Glory be to God for everything! Amen" on his lips.

Discuss

1. What did John Chrysostom's last name mean?
2. What was important to Chrysostom?

3. How was Chrysostom like Jesus?

4. How would you like to be more like Chrysostom and Jesus? What steps can you take today to begin?

Final Thought

If I were given a high position and the opportunity to spend time having fun with the rich and famous, I'm afraid I might go along with it. It takes great strength of character to turn away from these temptations and take the more difficult path of obedience. Chrysostom did just that. His love for God and love for others, especially those in need, compelled him to continue to preach and minister, even when it made important people angry.

Pray

Dear Lord Christ, give me such single-mindedness in my love for you and for others that I take the hard road of obedience. Amen.

Sing—*My Faith Looks Up to Thee* (p. 174)

May thy rich grace impart
Strength to my fainting heart,
My zeal inspire;
As thou hast died for me,
Oh, may my love to thee
Pure, warm, and changeless be,
A living fire!

Do

Place the symbol of John Chrysostom on your Tree of Saints.

Further Study for Adults

Read 1 John 3:16–20. How did Chrysostom put into practice these truths? What practical steps can you take to love the needy "with actions and in truth"?

OCTOBER 27

DAY 5

Augustine of Hippo is one of the best-known fathers of the early church. Through his writings, especially his *Confessions* and *The City of God,* Augustine has influenced Christian thought more than any other person since the apostles.

Augustine was born in North Africa, in the year A.D. 354. Augustine's father was a pagan, but his mother, Monica, was a devout Christian who brought him up in Scripture reading and prayer. When Augustine was a young man, however, he became involved in sinful living. This separated him from his mother and from the God of his childhood. An intelligent man with a hunger for truth, he explored many different philosophies and religions. Each of these ended in emptiness. Even though Augustine was a great teacher who enjoyed fame and success, inwardly, he was restless.

In 384, Augustine visited Milan, Italy, where he heard the preaching of Ambrose. This preaching had a tremendous impact on him. Once again, Augustine turned to the Bible, and God spoke to his heart. Suddenly Augustine understood what God had done for the world in Jesus Christ and how he needed to respond personally by confessing his sins and committing his life to God.

Augustine's life was changed. Monica was overjoyed to see her prayers for her son answered at last. Augustine was baptized by Ambrose on Easter eve, 387. He returned to his hometown of Hippo in 391 and was chosen by the townspeople to be a church leader. Four years later he was appointed bishop of Hippo. Augustine died of an illness on August 28, 430, at the age of seventy-five, as the Vandals were attacking the gates of the city of Hippo.

Discuss

1. How was Augustine raised?
2. What happened to the faith of his childhood when Augustine became a young man? Was he happy?

3. What led to Augustine's conversion?
4. How do you suppose God used Augustine's sinful past for good?

Final Thought

Once converted, Augustine's life was marked by a burning love for God. In fact, in later years, artists painted Augustine wearing the sign of a heart of fire. Perhaps because he had led such a wayward life, Augustine felt the joy of the forgiven sinner. As Jesus said, "He who has been forgiven little loves little" (Luke 7:47). Yet our sins are just as great as Augustine's were. Let us confess our sins each day and gladly receive God's forgiveness, so that we too might be filled with the love of God.

Pray

Lord, give us an awareness of our sins so that we can receive your grace and be filled with your love. Amen.

Sing—*Come Down, O Love Divine* (p. 170)

Come down, O Love divine;
Seek thou this soul of mine
And visit it with thine own ardor glowing;
O Comforter, draw near;
Within my heart appear
And kindle it, thy holy flame bestowing.

Do

Place the symbol of Augustine on your Tree of Saints.

Further Study for Adults

Read Luke 7:36–50. Which character in this story reminds you of Augustine? To which character can you best relate? What was the essential difference between Simon and the woman? How can you be more like the woman in this story?

OCTOBER 28

DAY 4

Martin Luther is one of the most important figures in church history. He has been called the Father of Protestantism, for before Luther, there was no Protestant church. Luther stands at a crossroad in the history of Christianity.

He was born in Eisleben, Germany in 1483 and as a young man began to study law. During a violent July thunderstorm, Luther was knocked from his horse by lightning and then and there vowed to become a monk. He entered a monastery, where he studied the Bible and wrote and taught, especially concentrating on the letters of Paul.

As he studied, he saw that the teachings of the church at that time were not in line with the Bible. The church emphasized that good works produced salvation. Luther could no longer accept this teaching because the Bible showed him that salvation comes by God's grace alone and that it is received by faith.

On October 31, 1517, Luther posted ninety-five theses (statements) on the door of the Castle Church in Wittenberg. These were copied and spread throughout Germany, causing an uproar of clashing ideas. The officials of the church did not like Martin Luther's ideas, because the ideas found fault with the officials and with their practices. They tried to make Luther recant, or go back on what he had said. Luther replied, "I am bound to the texts of the Bible, my conscience is captive to the Word of God. I neither can nor will recant anything, since it is neither right nor safe to act against conscience. God help me. Amen."

Discuss

1. What was Martin Luther's job as a priest?
2. What did he learn about salvation? What did he do about it?
3. What was the ultimate authority in Martin Luther's life?
4. How do we know what is true and right today?

Final Thought

Martin Luther was cut off from the Roman church. His followers started many churches, which became known as Lutheran churches. Luther's writings influenced many other Christian leaders of his day, who went on to establish other Protestant denominations. He did not want to start a big movement or become a famous person; he simply meant to stand for the truth as he saw it in the Word of God. Luther also wanted the common people to have the Bible in their own language so that they could understand it for themselves. The Bible at that time was only in Latin and so only could be read by the church officials, who had studied Latin. Therefore, Luther translated the entire Bible into German, the language of his own people.

Pray

Heavenly Father, thank you that you have given us your Word, and you have saved us by your grace alone in Jesus Christ. Amen.

Sing—*O Word of God Incarnate* (p. 177)

O Word of God incarnate,
O Wisdom from on high,
O Truth unchanged, unchanging,
O Light of our dark sky:
We praise you for the radiance
That from the hallowed page,
A lantern to our footsteps,
Shines on from age to age.

Do

Place the symbol of Martin Luther on your Tree of Saints.

Further Study for Adults

Read Romans 3:21–24 and Ephesians 2:4–10. How might these passages have been key in Martin Luther's doctrine of salvation? Define the terms *grace, faith,* and *works.* What difference has God's grace made in your life in the past? The present?

OCTOBER 29

DAY 3

John Calvin, born in France in 1509, is the father of the Presbyterian church. He followed Martin Luther in guiding the Protestant Reformation. Sometime between the ages of twenty and twenty-five, Calvin came to know Christ. About his conversion he wrote, "God at last turned my course in another direction by the secret rein of his providence." He began to study theology and write, producing many commentaries on books of the Bible.

At age twenty-five Calvin was forced to flee France because of persecution for his beliefs. He settled in Switzerland, where he continued to write, this time his famous *Institutes of the Christian Religion*.

On a trip to Strasbourg, he was forced to detour and spend a night in the city of Geneva. A Reformer in that city, Guillaume Farel, threatened Calvin with a curse from God unless he stay and help Farel reform the city and the church in Geneva. For two years Calvin stayed and labored, but the city did not want reformation. He and Farel were thrown out of the city in 1538.

Calvin moved to Strasbourg and pastored that city's French congregation. There he met and married the widow Idelette de Bure and spent the three best years of his life.

Calvin's friends gained control of Geneva and invited him back. For the next fourteen years, Calvin worked to make Geneva a city that honored God. Geneva became a safe haven for those fleeing religious persecution from the Roman church. Calvin believed that all of life should glorify God. He died in 1564, loved by his friends and scorned by his enemies.

Discuss

1. From what places was Calvin forced to leave? Why?
2. What were some of the jobs Calvin did during his life?
3. Which was the hardest for him? Which did he most enjoy?

4. Do you agree with Calvin that all of life should glorify God? Why or why not?

Final Thought

Calvin's followers wrote that the chief purpose of man is "to glorify God and enjoy him forever." What does this mean and how can we do this? To me, these words say that my life should point others to God in a way that honors God. That happens as I am like Jesus—loving, honest, and obedient to God. These words also say that I am to enjoy God. That means I take delight in spending time with him—in worship, in prayer, in studying his Word.

Pray

Dear Lord Jesus Christ, help me to glorify you and enjoy you. Let others see your presence in my life. Amen.

Sing—*All People That on Earth Do Dwell* (p. 168)

All people that on earth do dwell,
Sing to the Lord with cheerful voice;
Him serve with mirth, his praise forth tell;
Come ye before him and rejoice.

Do

Place the symbol of John Calvin on your Tree of Saints.

Further Study for Adults

Read Ephesians 1:3–14. Find all the occurrences of the words *praise*, *glory*, or *glorious* in this passage. How do these verses point to the "chief purpose of man"? Calvin also emphasized the doctrine of predestination in his preaching and writing. What do these verses teach about this subject? What was God's purpose in predestining us? How does your life measure up to this purpose?

OCTOBER 30

DAY 2

John and Charles Wesley, born in 1703 and 1707 respectively, were prominent figures in the beginnings of Methodism in England. They were two of nineteen children (only ten survived early childhood) and were raised in a very strict Anglican home by parents who both were devout and intelligent.

During their college years at Christ Church, Oxford, John and Charles formed "The Holy Club," a group of friends who met for prayer and for mutual encouragement in righteous living. After their ordination in 1735 they went to Savannah, Georgia, as missionaries to the American settlers. This period was marked by failure and personal struggles. Charles returned to England in 1736, John in 1738.

In May of 1738, they attended a meeting in Aldersgate Street not far from St. Paul's Cathedral in London. There they experienced an inner conversion. John was converted when he heard a reading of Luther's preface to the *Book of Romans*. John wrote, "I felt my heart strangely warmed. I felt I did trust in Christ, Christ alone, for salvation; and an assurance was given me that he had taken away my sins, even mine, and saved me from the law of sin and death."

Prior to this experience, John had never felt confident of his salvation and was always working hard to live a holy life. After his conversion, his preaching touched people's lives as it never before had. His followers, the Methodists, broke with the Church of England after the deaths of Charles in 1788 and John in 1799. Charles wrote over six thousand hymns, including "Hark! The Herald Angels Sing."

Discuss

1. What did John Wesley say about his conversion?
2. How was he different after this event?
3. Why do you suppose the Wesleys' efforts in Georgia were fruitless?

4. Are you confident of your salvation? Describe a life-changing experience you have had.

Final Thought

Elisabeth Elliot (see p. 58) tells about family devotions in her home growing up and the important place given to hymn singing. Her family sang their way through the hymnbook, from front to back, then began at the front again. Not only did they learn the hymns, but also they learned the great truths of the faith. Let's all take the time and effort to learn these songs that have stood the test of time.

Pray

Dear Lord, work in my heart so that I am truly changed. Teach me more about you, and fill me with love for you and for others. Amen.

Sing—*Love Divine, All Loves Excelling* (p. 173)

Love divine, all loves excelling,
Joy of heav'n, to earth come down!
Fix in us thy humble dwelling,
All thy faithful mercies crown.
Jesus, thou art all compassion,
Pure, unbounded love thou art;
Visit us with thy salvation,
Enter ev'ry trembling heart.

Do

Place the symbol of the Wesley brothers on your Tree of Saints.

Further Study for Adults

Are you confident of your salvation? What is the basis for your confidence? Using a concordance, find several passages that explain how we can know that we have eternal life.

OCTOBER 31

DAY 1

John Knox was an important figure in Scotland during the Reformation. He was a disciple of John Calvin and is one of the fathers of Presbyterianism in Scotland. Born in 1514, he became a Protestant through a Scottish preacher named George Wishart. When Wishart was burned at the stake in 1546, Protestants killed the Catholic leader who had sentenced him to death, and they seized St. Andrew's Castle on the North Sea. There they barricaded themselves in for safety from the Roman Catholics and remained for many months. They sent for John Knox to come and instruct them while they held the castle. When Knox preached, his zeal and his natural gifts were evident. He became the leader of the Protestants in Scotland.

Eventually the castle fell to the Roman Catholics. Knox was captured and sentenced to serve on the French galleys (ships that were propelled by oars). Nineteen months later Knox was released, thanks to influential English Protestants.

Knox spent time in England as a preacher, but his outspoken opinions made it necessary for him to flee to Geneva. There he saw the reforms that Calvin had made and was inspired to carry that vision to Scotland.

Knox was known for his plain speaking. He boasted that he "flattered no flesh." Even when he spoke face to face with Queen Mary, he did not say what she or anyone else wanted him to say. He spoke what he believed to be the simple truth. He was also known for acting on his beliefs, not just talking about them. Because of these two qualities, Knox made a lasting difference in the history of Great Britain and the Protestant movement. A leader in the Church of Scotland, he preached until his death in 1572.

Discuss

1. What happened to Knox's teacher, George Wishart?
2. How did Knox get to be a leader in the Church of Scotland?

3. For what qualities was Knox renowned?

4. Do you know anyone who possesses these qualities today? Do you admire this person? Why or why not?

Final Thought

John Knox was not a beautiful person. He was born into a working-class family, he was unattractive, and he never became a great scholar. He was aware of his shortcomings, yet he knew that God had called him. He saw himself as a "rude trumpet for God." So often I see my shortcomings and think that God can't possibly use me. I forget that God specializes in using those whom the world considers foolish or plain.

Pray

Thank you, O Lord, that you give each of us specific gifts as well as a job to do. Help us to offer you all that we are. Amen.

Sing—*The Church's One Foundation* (p. 169)

The Church's one foundation
Is Jesus Christ, her Lord;
She is his new creation
By water and the Word.
From heav'n he came and sought her
To be his holy bride;
With his own blood he bought her,
And for her life he died.

Do

Place the symbol of John Knox on your Tree of Saints.

Further Study for Adults

Read John 17. This passage was key in Knox's ideas about the church. What truths concerning the church do you glean from this chapter? Knox saw in these verses a church that was not a bureaucratic machine but rather a spiritual community. How can we be "in the world," yet avoid becoming "of the world"?

ALL SAINTS' DEVOTIONS: YEAR TWO

OCTOBER 22

DAY 10

William Carey has been called the Father of Modern Missions. Born in a poor English family in 1761, he was a very ordinary man whose unswerving commitment to God led him to greatness. Carey became a Christian in his teens. When he was almost twenty, he married Dorothy, a woman who never shared her husband's interest in world missions.

Carey's ideas about world missions sprang from reading *Captain Cook's Voyages*. As he pastored a Baptist church in England, he studied Scripture and became convinced that sending missionaries is the most important task of the church. It was while speaking to a group of Baptist ministers in 1792 that Carey said, "Expect great things from God; attempt great things for God." The next day, these ministers decided to organize what became the Baptist Missionary Society.

Carey volunteered to go to India as a missionary, but his wife refused to go. Later she unhappily agreed to join her husband. They went to the interior of India, where Dorothy and several of their children contracted malaria. When Peter, their five-year-old, died in 1794, Dorothy became mentally ill and never recovered.

Despite these family problems, Carey enjoyed great success as a missionary. He translated the entire Bible into three Indian languages, evangelized the Indians, and founded a college for training Indian converts in church planting and evangelism.

Six months after Dorothy's death in 1808, Carey remarried, this time happily. His new wife, Charlotte, helped him in his work and lovingly raised his sons. She died thirteen years later. Carey died in 1834.

Discuss

1. What were some of Carey's accomplishments?
2. What difficulties did he encounter?
3. How was Carey's marriage to Charlotte different from his marriage to Dorothy?
4. What lessons can we learn from Carey's life?

Final Thought

William Carey always overlooked the faults of others. It seemed he never had a bad word to say about anyone. This was a great help as he worked with other missionaries, for it enabled them to work together in harmony. He also respected the Indians' culture, which was quite a new idea. I admire these traits in Carey. I would like to become more respectful of others and more gracious in overlooking their weaknesses and faults.

Pray

Dear Lord Christ, thank you for William Carey's vision for world missions. Help me to be a missionary to my friends today. Amen.

Sing—*The Church's One Foundation* (p. 169)

The Church's one foundation
Is Jesus Christ, her Lord;
She is his new creation
By water and the Word.
From heav'n he came and sought her
To be his holy bride;
With his own blood he bought her,
And for her life he died.

Do

Place the symbol of William Carey on your Tree of Saints.

Further Study for Adults

Read Isaiah 54:2–3. This was the passage that Carey used as he preached to the Baptist ministers. How does his famous quotation relate to these verses? In what areas of your life do you need to "enlarge the place of your tent" and "stretch your tent curtains wide"? What great things can you expect God to do? Are there some great things that God is calling you to do?

OCTOBER 23

DAY 9

One of the greatest missionaries since the apostle Paul was Hudson Taylor, who lived from 1832 to 1905. His goal was to reach the four hundred million people of China with the gospel, and he developed a plan to do just that.

Taylor grew up in a Christian home in England, but he encountered Christ personally at the age of seventeen. Even as a small child, he had wanted to be a missionary to China; as a zealous new Christian, he determined to be one. He studied medicine, then in 1853 sailed for China.

Taylor was disappointed with the mission he found in Shanghai. He grew frustrated, homesick, and depressed. He began to strike out on his own, making trips into the interior of China. This he found exciting, but the Chinese were more interested in his strange clothing and hair than in his message. Taylor decided to adopt the dress and hairstyle of the Chinese so that his looks would not distract the Chinese. The other missionaries were apalled by this—they thought Taylor odd.

Taylor met Maria Dyer, who became his wife and true partner in ministry. During a furlough in England, Taylor recruited many men and women from the working class to come to China. People were moved by his passion for the Chinese people's souls. He spoke powerfully of "a million a month dying without God." This recruitment was the beginning of the China Inland Mission.

Discuss

1. What were the Chinese interested in when they saw Hudson Taylor?
2. Was this good or bad? What did Taylor do about it?
3. What drove Taylor to adopt a strange culture and work hard under very difficult circumstances?

4. Think for a moment about your goals. What drives you to work toward these goals?

Final Thought

Hudson Taylor was willing to be different and to endure ridicule in order to bring the good news of Christ to a lost people. His love for Christ and for the people of China translated into action. In our age of tolerance, we don't talk much about hell. Jesus did. If we really believe what Jesus said about the destiny of those who don't know him, we will work and pray to bring the gospel to others, near and far away.

Pray

Dear Lord, you desire that everyone come to know you. I pray now for _____ to come to you in faith. In Jesus' name, amen.

Sing—*O Zion, Haste* (p. 178)

O Zion, haste, your mission high fulfilling,
To tell to all the world that God is light;
That he who made all nations is not willing
One soul should perish, lost in shades of night.
Publish glad tidings, tidings of peace,
Tidings of Jesus, redemption, and release.

Do

Place the symbol of Hudson Taylor on your Tree of Saints.

Further Study for Adults

Read 1 Corinthians 9:19–23. How was Taylor like Paul in his approach? What adaptations can you make to communicate the gospel more effectively to friends and family who don't know Christ?

OCTOBER 24

DAY 8

Hudson and Maria Taylor returned to China in 1865 with their four children and fifteen untrained recruits to begin the work of the China Inland Mission. Almost immediately they ran into difficulties. Although the missionaries knew that they would have to adopt Chinese dress according to Taylor's practice, when it came right down to it, this proved too much for some of them. Several missionaries revolted, and it seemed that the small band of missionaries would be divided.

What saved the mission was the death of little Gracie, Taylor's beloved eight-year-old daughter. Her illness and death brought an outpouring of sympathy, which reunited the missionaries. Only three refused to come back in the fold, and they soon left the mission.

Taylor endured many other difficulties. Some of the Chinese people who were hostile to foreigners set fire to the mission house in Yangchow in 1868, and China Inland Mission was wrongly blamed for mistakes that British politicians made in handling this affair. As a result, supporters in England stopped sending money. The missionaries simply returned to the mission and continued their ministry. The rest of the Chinese community admired their courage and received them with open hearts.

The press and the British public attacked Taylor until he was almost at the point of a mental breakdown. He struggled with an overwhelming sense of sin and of failure. A caring friend shared with Taylor his own guiding principle in life: "To let my loving Savior work in me His will . . . Abiding, not striving or struggling . . ." As a result of this advice, Taylor was a new man. Soon after this turning point, two of Taylor's sons and his wife, Maria, died. His remaining three older children returned to England. Taylor remarried and continued evangelizing China until his death in 1905. Under Taylor's leadership, the China Inland Mission grew to include eight hundred missionaries.

Discuss

1. What difficult things happened to Hudson Taylor?
2. How do you think he felt when each of these things happened?
3. How did God use these difficulties for good?
4. How has God used very difficult times in your life to bring about his good purpose?

Final Thought

God spoke to Hudson Taylor through his friend. The message was exactly what Taylor desperately needed. Perhaps you know someone who, like Taylor, needs a word of encouragement today. Is there a missionary with whom you could correspond? Write about what God is teaching you, and God may use you as he did Hudson Taylor's friend.

Pray

Dear Lord Jesus, thank you that you give us friends to encourage us. Help us to encourage others, especially missionaries. Amen.

Sing—*O Zion, Haste* (p. 178)

Publish to ev'ry people, tongue, and nation
That God, in whom they live and move, is love;
Tell how he stooped to save his lost creation
And died on earth that we might live above.
Publish glad tidings, tidings of peace,
Tidings of Jesus, redemption, and release.

Do

Place the symbol of China on your Tree of Saints.

Further Study for Adults

Taylor's friend also wrote, "Not a striving to have faith or to increase our faith, but a looking at the Faithful One seems all we need." What does this mean? Read Ephesians 2:8 and Hebrews 12:2. What bearing do these verses have on this subject? How do we "fix our eyes on Jesus"?

OCTOBER 25

DAY 7

Lottie Moon, born in Virginia in 1840, has been called the Patron Saint of Southern Baptist Missions. Her father died when she was twelve, but her mother reared the seven children in an atmosphere of deep faith. Lottie strayed from her faith as a college student, but God touched her heart at a campus revival meeting. Trained as a school teacher, Lottie taught in Carters-ville, Georgia, but this job did not satisfy her desire for Christian service and adventure. In 1872, her sister Edmonia went as a missionary to China. Within one year, Lottie joined her. Edmonia did not fare well as a missionary and four years later returned home to Virginia. After her sister left, Lottie slid into depression and loneliness.

Lottie's loneliness was made all the more painful by a broken heart. Her boyfriend, Crawford Toy, a professor at a Southern Baptist seminary, asked her to marry him and go with him to Japan, where they could serve as missionaries together. Only one thing held Lottie back; she knew that Toy believed in Darwin's theory of evolution. She researched the theory, believed it to be wrong, and decided that this issue was important enough to prevent her from marrying Toy. Years later someone asked Lottie if she had ever been in love. She answered, "Yes, but God had first claim on my life, and since the two conflicted, there could be no question about the result."

Discuss

1. Why was Lottie lonely?
2. What difficult choice did Lottie have to make? What made this decision so difficult?
3. Why did Lottie decide not to marry Crawford Toy?
4. What was Lottie's "bottom line"? What is your bottom line?

Final Thought

Even when loneliness almost overwhelmed her, Lottie did not give up. She persevered. When marriage to an intelligent and attractive man promised a lifetime of companionship, Lottie was careful to listen for God's voice. She heard God telling her no. So Lottie obeyed God and took the hard road of obedience. Are you willing to stay in a hard and lonely place out of obedience to God?

Pray

Dear Lord, thank you for the example of Lottie Moon. Help me, like her, to obey you even when it is difficult. Amen.

Sing—*O Jesus, I Have Promised* (p. 176)

O Jesus, I have promised
To serve you to the end;
Remain forever near me,
My master and my friend.
I shall not fear the battle
If you are by my side,
Nor wander from the pathway
If you will be my guide.

Do

Place the symbol of Lottie Moon on your Tree of Saints.

Further Study for Adults

Read Luke 14:25–33. How might God have used these verses to speak to Lottie in her time of decision? Summarize Jesus' main point. Is there something or someone that you love more than Christ? How can you give up everything for his sake? Are there some specific steps God is calling you to take today?

OCTOBER 26

DAY 6

Lottie continued her work in China. She wanted to evangelize China, yet she found herself restricted to teaching. She grew increasingly frustrated with simply teaching forty Chinese girls who were not interested in learning. Lottie wrote, "Can we wonder at the mortal weariness and disgust, the sense of wasted powers and the conviction that her life is a failure, that comes over a woman when, instead of the ever broadening activities she had planned, she finds herself tied down to the petty work of teaching a few girls. . . . What women want who come to China is free opportunity to do the largest possible work. . . . What women have a right to demand is perfect equality."

Such words, written in magazine articles, created quite a reaction. Eventually, Lottie had the opportunity she had so long desired. Three men from a nearby village appeared at her door wanting her to come and tell about this new doctrine. She went with them, and was delighted at what she found: "Something I had never seen before in China . . . Such eagerness to learn! Such spiritual desires!" She planted a church in that village, and twenty years later the Chinese pastor of that church had baptized more than two thousand new Chinese Christians.

During the last twenty-two years of her life, Lottie divided her time between evangelistic work in the Chinese villages and training new missionaries in Tengchow. She wrote extensively, kindling a passion for foreign missions in the hearts of Southern Baptist women. Famine and uprising brought mass starvation in Tengchow in 1911. Lottie gave all that she had to help others. She herself starved to death. The *Foreign Missions Journal* wrote that she was "the best man among our missionaries."

Discuss

1. What was it that Lottie wanted to do as a missionary?
2. Why was she not allowed to do this?

3. What eventually happened to change her ministry?

4. What does Lottie's death demonstrate about the kind of person she was?

Final Thought

Success or failure? Lottie Moon's life and death make us wonder what we mean by these words. She evangelized thousands, started churches, and raised support for and awareness of missions. These achievements sound like success. She died of starvation, penniless, alone, far from her home in Virginia. This sounds like failure. I believe that God counts success not by what we achieve but by what we give. Lottie gave all she had, in life and in death.

Pray

Dear Lord Jesus, you gave yourself completely for me. Help me to give all that I am and have to you, for your service. Amen.

Sing—*My Faith Looks Up to Thee* (p. 174)

May thy rich grace impart
Strength to my fainting heart,
My zeal inspire;
As thou hast died for me,
Oh, may my love to thee
Pure, warm, and changeless be,
A living fire!

Do

Place the symbol of the Chinese villagers on your Tree of Saints.

Further Study for Adults

Read Matthew 16:24–28. Here is another of Jesus' teachings about self-denial and the cross. Lottie Moon certainly did not take these passages to mean that she should turn into a doormat. How do you interpret these verses? How are we to deny ourselves? What is God calling you to deny?

OCTOBER 27

DAY 5

Like Lottie Moon, Amy Carmichael was a single woman missionary whose unswerving commitment and untiring service made a permanent mark on the kingdom of God. Amy was born in Northern Ireland in 1867 and in her late teens began mission work in the inner city of Belfast among the girls who worked at the mills and factories.

At the age of twenty-four, Amy received what she described as a "call from God" to go to the foreign mission field. Her faith was such that she had no choice but to obey. She went to Japan. There she encountered disappointment and difficulty. Her health, both physical and mental, suffered. After fifteen months, she left Japan for Ceylon, believing that God was leading her there. After a brief furlough to Ireland, she returned to the mission field, this time to India. It was in India that Amy spent the rest of her days.

Amy, again like Lottie Moon, struggled with loneliness, especially as she anticipated the future as a single woman. As she turned to God with everything else, so she turned to God with her loneliness. Amy wrote that God responded to her by saying, *None of them that trust in me shall be desolate.*

Amy walked closely with her Lord and believed that she had a direct line of communication with him. While some doubted and disapproved of this claim, Amy's character certainly reflected the character of Jesus. Sherwood Eddy, a fellow missionary and author who knew her well, wrote of her, "Miss Carmichael was a blessing to all who came into intimate and understanding contact with her radiant life. . . . Amy Wilson Carmichael was the most Christlike character I ever met, and . . . her life was the most fragrant, the most joyfully sacrificial, that I ever knew."

Discuss

1. What kind of a person was Amy Carmichael?

2. How was she different from most of the people you know?
3. Can you remember a time when you were certain that God was speaking to you? What did he say?
4. What can you do to be able to hear God's voice more clearly?

Final Thought

Many Christian leaders claim to hear God's voice. The Bible says, "By their fruit you will recognize them" (Matt. 7:16). That means that people's lives—their actions and their attitudes—show what is in their hearts. Amy's life was a continual outpouring of love. She showed by her actions that she had the heart of Jesus Christ.

Pray

Dear Lord, change my heart to be like Jesus' heart: filled with love for you and for others. Help me to show that love in all that I do and say. Amen.

Sing—*Come Down, O Love Divine* (p. 170)

Come down, O Love divine;
Seek thou this soul of mine
And visit it with thine own ardor glowing;
O Comforter, draw near;
Within my heart appear
And kindle it, thy holy flame bestowing.

Do

Place the symbol of Amy Carmichael on your Tree of Saints.

Further Study for Adults

Read John 15:1–17. This was a passage that Amy Carmichael loved. What does it mean to remain in Jesus? What are God's desires and goals for us, according to these verses? What specific commands are we given? What specific actions can you take today to begin to conform to God's purposes?

OCTOBER 28

DAY 4

Amy's ministry in India centered on children. The Hindu people in southern India had a terrible secret practice of selling children into slavery to the Hindu temple. The children were then used for the evil pleasures of the Hindu men who came to worship there. Amy began a rescue operation, using converted Indian women as spies. Within twelve years, Amy had rescued 130 children. This was a dangerous business. Several times she was charged with kidnapping. Often her very life was in danger, because the Hindu priests and men didn't like what she was doing.

Amy began a community, which she called Dohnavur Fellowship, to care for these children. Western missionaries and Indian staff workers lived and worked together, all wearing Indian dress. At Dohnavur, the children received education, physical care, and moral training in addition to spiritual instruction.

Some people in the British Isles felt that she paid too much attention to educating and caring for the children and not enough attention to evangelizing them. To this Amy responded, "One cannot save and then pitchfork souls into heaven. . . . Souls are more or less securely fastened to bodies . . . and as you cannot get the souls out and deal with them separately, you have to take them both together."

Hundreds of children were rescued from misery and introduced to Jesus Christ by the efforts of Amy Carmichael. She died at Dohnavur in 1951 at the age of eighty-three.

Discuss

1. What did Amy do in India?
2. Who didn't like what she was doing?
3. What can you tell about Amy's character by the ministry that she undertook?
4. What about Amy do you most admire?

Final Thought

Few Christian leaders or missionaries have Amy Carmichael's heart for children. In this love for children it seems to me Amy certainly demonstrated the character of Christ. Jesus had a special concern for children. He welcomed them when the disciples wanted to send them away, and he strictly warned those who would lead children into sin. Amy spent her life rescuing children out of darkness. How happy this must have made the Lord.

Pray

Dear Lord Jesus, thank you for your care for helpless children. Protect those who are in trouble. Show us what we can do to rescue them as Amy did. Amen.

Sing—*Praise, My Soul, the King of Heaven* (p. 179)

Tenderly he shields and spares us;
Well our feeble frame he knows.
In his hands he gently bears us,
Rescues us from all our foes.
Alleluia! Alleluia!
Widely as his mercy flows.

Do

Place the symbol of the Indian girl on your Tree of Saints.

Further Study for Adults

Read 1 John 4:7–12. Write these verses out in your own words. How did Amy Carmichael exemplify the truths of these verses? Pray for God to show you opportunities to demonstrate his love to others. Then keep your eyes open and be ready to respond.

OCTOBER 29

DAY 3

William Cameron Townsend was called by Billy Graham "the greatest missionary of our time." He was the driving force behind the Bible translation work that has brought Scripture to the farthest ends of the earth in the past fifty years.

Cam Townsend was born in California in 1896. During his college years he felt called to missions. He volunteered as a Bible salesman to Latin America and was assigned to Guatemala. His work took him to areas where the people spoke a language that had never been written. These people were uninterested in his Spanish Bibles. One day a man challenged Cam, "Why, if your God is so smart, hasn't he learned our language?"

This led Cam to spend the next thirteen years learning their language. By the time he completed the New Testament in Cakchiquel, Cam was firmly committed to the importance of Bible translation work.

The mission organization Cam was with wanted him to stay with the Cakchiquel Indians, but Cam felt led to continue in translation work with other language groups. He and a friend founded Camp Wycliffe in Arkansas, a school to teach missionaries linguistics to prepare for Bible translation. This became Wycliffe Bible Translators, which is the world's largest independent Protestant mission organization.

Cam was very open-minded. He supported participation in Wycliffe by Christians of many different persuasions, which angered some of the organization's members and supporters. "Uncle Cam," as he was called, loved to say, "The greatest missionary is the Bible in the Mother tongue. It never needs a furlough, is never considered an outsider." Cam Townsend died in 1982 at the age of eighty-six.

Discuss

1. What gave Cam the idea of translating the Bible?
2. Why was this such a good idea?
3. What difference would it make in your life if you did not have the Bible in your own language?

4. Why do you suppose Billy Graham called Cam the greatest missionary of our time?

Final Thought

After Wycliffe was founded, Cam went on to establish the Summer Institute of Linguistics (SIL). Everyone assumed that he would be the director, but he refused. He thought that it was dangerous for one man to have control of an organization. Instead he turned the control over to a committee and said that he would serve under their authority and that of the membership. This meant that many times Cam did not get his way. What a wise and humble man!

Pray

Dear Lord, thank you for giving Cam Townsend the vision for translating the Bible into every language. Help me to read and obey your Word and spread it to those around me. Amen.

Sing—*O Word of God Incarnate* (p. 177)

O Word of God incarnate,
O Wisdom from on high,
O Truth unchanged, unchanging,
O Light of our dark sky:
We praise you for the radiance
That from the hallowed page,
A lantern to our footsteps,
Shines on from age to age.

Do

Place the symbol of Cam Townsend on your Tree of Saints.

Further Study for Adults

Read 2 Timothy 3:14–17. Why might these verses have meant a great deal to Cam? What does Scripture do in our lives? What is its ultimate purpose? What can you do to benefit more from your study of God's Word?

OCTOBER 30

DAY 2

One of the most well-known missionary endeavors in modern times is the attempt of Jim Elliot, Pete Fleming, Ed McCully, Nate Saint, and Roger Youderian to reach the hostile Auca Indians in the jungle of Ecuador. These tribespeople had killed dozens, if not hundreds, of outsiders before the five missionaries decided to evangelize them in 1955. These zealous young men hoped that their work would be one of the greatest missionary breakthroughs of their time.

They began by dropping gifts for the Aucas as they flew over the Auca village in a small plane (Nate was a jungle pilot). Then they flew over the villages and lowered a bucket with gifts. Much to their delight, the Aucas returned the bucket filled with gifts for them: a live parrot, peanuts, and a smoked monkey tail. The missionaries regarded these gifts as expressions of friendship and felt that the time had come to make face-to-face contact.

On January 3, 1956, Nate began to ferry the other men to a river-bank landing strip near Auca territory. He joined them, and for several days they waited for the Aucas to appear. On January 7, the Aucas arrived and speared all five missionaries to death.

The Aucas were not forgotten. Other missionaries continued to drop gifts. Rachel Saint, sister of Nate, had been studying the Auca language. She continued to learn the language, and she and Elisabeth Elliot, Jim's widow, along with baby Valerie Elliot, were invited to live with the tribe only two and a half years after the missionaries' murder. They translated the Bible into the Auca language and saw the killers of their loved ones come to Christ.

Discuss

1. How did the missionaries try to make friends with the Aucas?
2. Did it work? Why do you think the Aucas killed them?

3. With what thoughts and feelings do you suppose the wives and families of these men struggled?
4. What can you tell about the character of Rachel Saint and Elisabeth Elliot from this account?

Final Thought

Jim Elliot is famous for saying, "He is no fool who gives what he cannot keep to gain what he cannot lose." In other words, if we live for our own happiness, we will never be happy. But if we give up our own selfish desires and live to please Jesus Christ, we will have rich rewards in heaven as well as true joy on earth. Jim and his friends gave their lives for Christ. Not only are they enjoying eternal life with Jesus, but the story of their sacrifice has brought thousands of people around the world to a deep commitment to Christ.

Pray

Dear Lord, take all that I am and make me yours forever. Amen.

Sing—*O Word of God Incarnate* (p. 177)

The Church from you, dear Master,
Received the gift divine;
And still that light is lifted
O'er all the earth to shine.
It is the chart and compass
That, all life's voyage through,
Mid mists and rocks and quicksands
Still guides, O Christ, to you.

Do

Place the symbol of the Auca Indian on your Tree of Saints.

Further Study for Adults

Read Matthew 16:24–26. Jim Elliot's words are really a paraphrase of this verse. What do you think it means to lose your life for Christ's sake?

OCTOBER 31

DAY 1

Mother Teresa is a modern-day saint and missionary who at the time of this writing is still living. She was born in Yugoslavia in 1910 and at the age of twelve felt called by God to be a missionary to the poor. She became a nun in the Roman Catholic church at age eighteen, and when she learned about a work in India, she offered to go.

She went to Calcutta, where the desperate poverty there moved her to action. Not willing to stay in a convent, Mother Teresa began to go among the sick and dying and minister to those whom she called "the poorest of the poor." She established the Missionaries of Charity for the purpose of bringing Christ's love to these folk. This sisterhood has been established in cities all over the world, staffed largely by Indian nuns whose lives have been touched by Christ in Mother Teresa.

Mother Teresa wrote:

> Our progress in holiness depends on God and ourselves—on God's grace and on our will to be holy. We must have a real living determination to reach holiness. "I will be a saint" means I will despoil myself of all that is not God; I will strip my heart of all created things; I will live in poverty and detachment; I will renounce my will, my inclinations, my whims and fancies, and make myself a willing slave to the will of God. . . . True holiness consists in doing God's will with a smile.

Recently Mother Teresa visited Washington, D.C. Her message at the National Prayer Breakfast challenged us to love our elderly parents and to love our children, born and unborn. People listen to her because she has lived out her message.

Discuss

1. What does Mother Teresa do in India and around the world?
2. Describe an experience you have had with someone who was very poor. What feelings did you have at the time?

3. How does Mother Teresa define sainthood?

4. What do you need to renounce in order to grow in holiness?

Final Thought

We often think that we need nice things and comforts to be happy. Mother Teresa shows us the path to true joy. She wrote:

> We have it in our power to be in heaven with him right now—to be happy with him at this very moment. But being happy with him now means: loving as he loves, helping as he helps, giving as he gives, serving as he serves, rescuing as he rescues, being with him twenty-four hours, touching him in his distressing disguise.

Pray

Dearest Lord, give me eyes to see you in the hurting people all around me. Give me strength and courage to serve you by sacrificing my comforts to help those in need. Amen.

Sing—*O Zion, Haste* (p. 178)

O Zion, haste, your mission high fulfilling,
To tell to all the world that God is light;
That he who made all nations is not willing
One soul should perish, lost in shades of night.
Publish glad tidings, tidings of peace,
Tidings of Jesus, redemption, and release.

Do

Place the symbol of Mother Teresa on your Tree of Saints.

Further Study for Adults

Read Matthew 25:31–46. What are some modern-day examples of "the least of these" or in Mother Teresa's words, "the poorest of the poor"? What can your family do to begin to minister to the needy in your community?

ALL SAINTS' PARTY

C hildren love to dress up in costumes, play games, win prizes, and get lots of goodies. That is why Halloween holds such attraction for them. However, a fun party can incorporate all these elements without the ghosts and witches theme. Any alternative to Halloween needs to be just as much fun as Halloween—or more so.

Parties are becoming more and more common on Halloween because parents are reluctant to send their children out trick-or-treating in this day of increased violence. Because of this trend, children will not be branded as "weird" for going to an All Saints' party instead of going trick-or-treating. And if they have more fun and get more goodies than all their friends, they will feel that they got the better end of the stick.

An All Saints' party revolves around Bible heroes and godly men and women in church history instead of around the evil characters that generally figure into Halloween. Invite several other Christian families to participate with you in this event. They will be comfortable with the biblical theme and will probably appreciate having an alternative to the usual Halloween activities.

Making It Fun

A fun party consists of good friends, good food, and fun activities. These elements require some careful planning but need not be costly or overly involved. Several suggestions follow that may help you plan your All Saints' party. Perhaps these will spark your imagination to create something that your family will enjoy even more than traditional Halloween events.

Good Food. Spread your table with treats to eat during the party, either throughout the evening (finger foods) or at a specific time (cake and ice cream).

Goody Bags. Make sure that the children take home a goody bag full of treats so that they don't wish that they had been able to go out trick-or-treating. (Most kids evaluate the success of their evening by dumping the contents of their goody bag on the floor and proceeding to count the various treats.)

Costumes. Children delight in dressing up. For an All Saints' party they dress up as Bible characters. Animals—from the creation,

Noah's ark, and a host of other Bible stories in which animals play a part—qualify as Bible characters. As the children make their initial appearances in their costumes, they should be made to feel that their own costume is something special. Avoid contests for best costumes—this leads to disappointment for many.

Storytelling. Scour your church or public library for stories of great Christians. Find a story that is the appropriate length and level for the ages of children present, one that will excite and inspire them. Look for stories about such saints as Martin Luther, Hudson Taylor, Amy Carmichael, or the Wesleys. Foxe's *Book of Martyrs* is jam-packed with harrowing tales of those who laid down their lives for Jesus Christ. Schedule a story time in the events of the evening and read the account dramatically.

Games. Plan a number of simple, fun party games. These can be ordinary party games or they can be slightly modified to capitalize on the Bible hero theme. The emphasis here is not on learning, although in some cases learning may result. Rather, the emphasis is on hilarity—just plain fun!

Here are several examples of ordinary party games that have been modified to reflect the theme of Bible characters and events:

Abraham's Walk of Faith

Materials: Blindfolds

Location: Outdoors in yard or indoors, using entire house

Time: About 10 minutes

Object of the Game: To learn to trust another person by following his voice without being able to see.

To Play: Divide the group into pairs. In each pair, one will be the follower and the other will be the leader. The follower puts on a blindfold and cannot see anything. First, have the leader spin the follower around so that the follower is disoriented. Then, the leader must lead the follower around the yard or house using only verbal directions. The older the players, the more complex and circuitous a route they should take. When the leader has returned to the starting point with the follower, the follower should take off the blindfold.

Have the follower guess where the route led. Then switch places, the leader becoming the follower and vice versa.

Note: Emphasize that it is extremely important for the leader to be trustworthy. All players must be willing and able to lead their partners so that the followers do not hurt themselves. If some of the children are unable to handle this responsibility, use a different game.

Eye Spy

Explain: There are spies in the Bible! The most famous spy was Joshua, who, with Caleb and ten other spies, scouted out Canaan before the Israelites entered.

Number of Players: 5–25

Time: 15–60 minutes

Materials: One candle, a dark room, a slip of paper for each player

Object of the Game: To guess which player is the spy before you are winked at by the spy

To Play: On one of the slips of paper, draw an eye. Leave the other slips of paper blank or draw an X on them. Fold up the slips of paper and put them in a bowl or basket.

Have all the players sit in one circle around a lighted candle. Turn out all the other lights. Pass the bowl around and have each player select a slip of paper. The one who selects the slip with the eye on it is the spy.

Once everyone has looked at his or her slip and folded it back up, playing commences. All players must maintain eye contact with other players at all times during this game. The spy gets players out by winking at them. The spy tries to get as many players out as possible before someone guesses that he or she is the spy. The players try to guess who is the spy before the spy catches their eye, winks at them, and they are out.

If a player sees another player wink and suspects him of being the spy, that player says "Eye Spy!" and indicates who the spy is. The accused spy must show his slip of paper to prove his guilt or innocence. If the guess is wrong, the player who guessed is out. If the guess is right, the player who guessed wins the game, and a second round may begin.

Heroes of the Faith Charades

Number of Players: Any number
Time: 15–60 minutes
Materials: A Bible
Object of the Game: To guess which Bible character is being portrayed by the actor.

To Play: Each player is given a turn to be the actor. The actor selects a hero of the faith either from the Bible or from church history and has three minutes to convey (without words) the identity of this character. The actor can do this by pantomiming scenes from this character's life or by using charades techniques (holding up two fingers means the name has two syllables; cupping the ear means "sounds like," etc.) to communicate the character's name. Other players, of course, must try to guess the character. The person with the right answer takes the next turn unless he or she has already had a turn. If so, that person may give the turn to someone who has not yet been the actor.

Hero Interviews

Number of Players: Any number
Length of Time: 10–20 minutes
Materials: A tape recorder and a blank tape
Object of the Game: To identify with Bible characters and make them come alive by using a man-on-the-street interview routine

To Play: Each player selects a Bible character to represent. One of the older children is the "roving reporter." (Several may take turns at being the reporter. It helps if the reporter is a bit of a ham!) Each Bible character is interviewed by the reporter, who is taping the interview. Here is a sample interview:

Reporter:	I have with me today David of Bethlehem, who has just killed Goliath and won a major victory for Israel. Tell me, David, how did you, a shepherd boy, end up fighting against the giant Philistine?
David:	Well, I was bringing some cheese to my brothers, who are in the army. When I got to the battlefield, I couldn't believe my ears. This big bully was calling the Israelites names and making fun of the one true God. I was pretty upset. I told King Saul that I would fight against Goliath and show the Philistines whose God is the real one.
Reporter:	Were you nervous?
David:	Not really. You see, as a shepherd, I've come up against some pretty scary things—lions and bears after my sheep. God has given me the power to fight these beasts with my bare hands and tear them limb from limb. I knew that he would deliver Goliath into my hands.
Reporter:	How did you know that?
David:	I just knew that God wouldn't stand for his name being dragged in the mud by those wicked, filthy Philistines.
Reporter:	I heard that King Saul offered you the use of his armor.
David:	Yeah, that was pretty funny. I put on his armor and it was so heavy, I couldn't move. I would have been a sitting duck in that.
Reporter:	Tell our listeners about your weapon, David.
David:	I went to the brook and picked out five smooth stones. I had my slingshot, and all it took was one— plop! right in the forehead, and down went Goliath.

Reporter:	Pretty good shot, I'd say, and very courageous, David.
David:	Hey, it wasn't me—it was the Lord who won that battle.
Reporter:	Thank you for your time, David. I think that we may see more of this young hero in the years ahead.

As the reporter interviews a character, all the other players sit around and watch. Essentially, it is a skit, with everyone taking turns participating and with the tape recorder as the prop that pulls it together.

Obviously, this game works best with older elementary children, most of whom seem to have a flair for the dramatic. Very young children will clam up entirely. Children in the primary grades may have fun with this game, as long as they are allowed to do it their way and are free not to participate if they should so choose.

If the children know about this well ahead of time, they will research their parts by reading time-worn Bible stories with new eyes. This game forces them to probe Bible characters and imagine what it was like to be them. It also encourages the children to learn and remember the details of the biblical accounts.

Numerous other games can be similarly modified to incorporate biblical themes. "Pin the Tail on the Donkey" can become "Pin the Tail on Balaam's Donkey." (Many will be surprised to know that the Bible tells of a time when a donkey actually talked. Ask the children how many believe that there is such a story in the Bible. You can find the account in Numbers 22.) A bean bag toss can be called "Clobber Goliath," with a drawing of a large, ugly face for the target. Indoor or outdoor relay races can reflect the race between Elijah and Ahab (see 1 Kings 18:44–46). The possibilities are endless. Let your imagination and the personality of your family be your guides as you begin a new family tradition for celebrating the eve of All Saints' Day.

ALL SAINTS' FAMILY CELEBRATION

Family Worship on All Saints' Day

Call to Worship

Leader: Almighty God, you have made all Christians a part of the body of your Son Jesus Christ our Lord. We share in this fellowship with those who now worship you in heaven. Today we remember those who have gone before us into your presence. Give us grace to follow the examples of godly men and women, so that we too may experience the joy that comes in loving you. We pray this in the name of the living Lord Jesus Christ. Amen.

Responsive Reading (Adapted from Hebrews 11)

(Note: R1 stands for Reader 1, etc.)

R1: Now faith is being sure of what we hope for and certain of what we do not see.

All: Lord, grant us faith.

R2: By faith we understand that the universe was formed at God's command.

All: Lord, grant us faith.

R3: By faith, Abel offered a better sacrifice than Cain did.

All: Lord, grant us faith.

R4: By faith, Enoch was taken from this life and did not experience death.

All: Lord, grant us faith.

R1: By faith, Noah, when warned about things not yet seen, in holy fear built an ark.

All: Lord, grant us faith.

R2: By faith, Abraham, when called to go to a place he would later receive as his inheritance, obeyed and went, even though he did not know where he was going.

All: Lord, grant us faith.

R3:   By faith Abraham, even though he was old—and Sarah herself was barren—was enabled to become a father because he considered him faithful who had made the promise.

All: Lord, grant us faith.

R4:   By faith Abraham, when God tested him, offered Isaac as a sacrifice.

All: Lord, grant us faith.

R1:   By faith Isaac blessed Jacob and Esau in regard to their future.

All: Lord, grant us faith.

R2:   By faith Jacob, when he was dying, blessed each of Joseph's sons, and worshiped God.

All: Lord, grant us faith.

R3:   By faith Joseph, when his end was near, spoke about the exodus of the Israelites from Egypt and gave instructions about his bones.

All: Lord, grant us faith.

R4:   By faith Moses' parents hid him for three months after his birth.

All: Lord, grant us faith.

R1:   By faith Moses left Egypt, not fearing the king's anger; he persevered because he saw the One who is invisible.

All: Lord, grant us faith.

R2:   By faith Moses kept the Passover.

All: Lord, grant us faith.

R3:   By faith the people passed through the Red Sea as on dry land.

All: Lord, grant us faith.

R4:   By faith the walls of Jericho fell, after the people had marched around them for seven days.

All: Lord, grant us faith.

R1:   By faith the prostitute Rahab, because she welcomed the spies, was not killed with those who were disobedient.

All: Lord, grant us faith.

R2:   And what more shall I say? I do not have time to tell about Gideon, Barak, Samson, Jephthah, David, Samuel, and the prophets, who through faith conquered kingdoms, administered justice, and gained what was promised; who shut the mouths of lions, quenched the fury of the flames, and escaped the edge of the sword; whose weakness was turned to strength; and who became powerful in battle and routed foreign armies (Heb. 11:32–34).

R3:   Women received back their dead, raised to life again. Others were tortured and refused to be released, so that they might gain a better resurrection. Some faced jeers and flogging, while still others were chained and put in prison. They were stoned; they were sawed in two; they were put to death by the sword. They went about in sheepskins and goatskins, destitute, persecuted and mistreated—the world was not worthy of them (vv. 35–38a).

R4:   They wandered in deserts and mountains, and in caves and holes in the ground. These were all commended for their faith, yet none of them received what had been promised. God had planned something better for us so that only together with us would they be made perfect (vv. 38b–40).

R1:   Therefore, since we are surrounded by such a great cloud of witnesses, let us throw off everything that hinders and the sin that so easily entangles, and let us run with perseverance the race marked out for us. Let us fix our eyes on Jesus, the author and perfecter of our faith, who for the joy set before him endured the cross, scorning its shame, and sat down at the right hand of the throne of God (12:1–2).

Leader: Today we remember men and women whose lives of faith serve as a shining beacon to us. Let's take some time to tell about the people who have helped us come to know Jesus Christ and grow in our faith in him. (Each member who is able and willing has an opportunity now to share his or her story of faith.)

Sing—*O Zion, Haste* (p. 178)

O Zion, haste, your mission high fulfilling,
To tell to all the world that God is light;
That he who made all nations is not willing
One soul should perish, lost in shades of night.
Publish glad tidings, tidings of peace,
Tidings of Jesus, redemption, and release.

Publish to ev'ry people, tongue, and nation
That God, in whom they live and move, is love;
Tell how he stooped to save his lost creation
And died on earth that we might live above.
Publish glad tidings, tidings of peace,
Tidings of Jesus, redemption, and release.

Leader: Heavenly Father, we thank you for the men and women who have followed you faithfully throughout the centuries. Thank you for the sacrifices that they made so that we might know the one true God and Jesus Christ, his Son. Help us now run that race with perseverance, keeping our eyes fixed on Jesus, in whose name we pray. Amen.

THANKSGIVING THEN AND NOW

T wenty kindergarteners stood in one long, disheveled row, bedecked in Pilgrim hats and Indian headdresses made from colorful construction paper. Their parents sat awkwardly in tiny chairs at tiny tables, eyes glued to their own little cherubs. An aura of joyful festivity filled the room. With some prompting from the teachers, the children proudly sang their song about turkeys, complete with hand motions.

It was Miss Martin's annual Thanksgiving feast. The children were the Pilgrim and Indian hosts and served their parents a delicious Thanksgiving meal (dishes prepared and brought by the parents, of course). Several parents spooned the food onto plates that the children held and then set before their parents. Having been through this procedure the last year with my son, Mark, I was an old hand and thus qualified as a server.

Soon the plates were all filled and the children sat beside their parents at the miniature tables, poised to dive into the food. There was a brief, uncomfortable silence.

"Children, it's Thanksgiving! What do we say to the parents who brought these good things?" prompted the teacher.

"Thank you!" the children cried in unison. Everyone commenced eating; the tension lifted.

How sad, I thought to myself. It would have been most appropriate to say a prayer. After all, that is what Thanksgiving is all about—thanking God for his care for us. But our culture has shut God out of Thanksgiving as it has shut him out of the rest of public life.

The First Thanksgiving?

If you think that Thanksgiving began with the Pilgrims, guess again! The Thanksgiving holiday finds its true roots in the earliest pages of human history.

Eve gave thanks to God when she gave birth to Cain. Later, the naming of Seth was a tribute of thanksgiving to the God who provides. God's people offered sacrifices to God, not only in repentance for sin, but also in thanksgiving to and worship of God. When Noah emerged from the ark, he immediately erected an altar and offered a sacrifice of thanksgiving to God.

God himself instituted three yearly thanksgiving festivals to be observed by the Israelites. These festivals were a part of the law that God gave Moses on Mount Sinai (see Exod. 23:14–17). The first was the Feast of Unleavened Bread, commemorating God's deliverance of Israel from bondage in Egypt. The second was the Feast of Harvest, a festival of joy upon reaping the first fruits of the crops. The third thanksgiving feast was the Feast of Ingathering, which celebrated the ingathering of the crops at the end of the harvest as well as God's provision during Israel's years of wandering in the desert. Three times each year, Israel was to celebrate God's goodness with a feast of thanksgiving.

A spirit of thanksgiving characterized the early church. As the Holy Spirit touched the lives of men and women and they realized what Jesus had done for them, their hearts overflowed with gratitude. The theme of thankfulness to God through our Lord Jesus Christ permeates the Epistles. From Genesis to Revelation, the people of God were people who gave thanks and praise to him.

Now to the Mayflower

The courageous Christians who journeyed to the New World on the tiny *Mayflower* also trusted the God of the Scriptures. The Pilgrims came seeking freedom to worship God. They left home, family, and security, risking their very lives for this freedom.

After an arduous transatlantic voyage, they landed in early December 1620, ill prepared to face a winter in the New England wilderness. Despite relatively mild weather, half of the colonists died during those first few months.

When spring finally arrived, the small group of survivors planted crops and began to build. The Native Americans befriended them and taught them how to catch fish and plant corn. By harvest, they were established and prepared to meet the onslaught of winter. God had protected them and provided for their needs. A feast of thanksgiving was their response to God's goodness and providence.

The Pilgrims must have been thankful for many things: an abundant harvest, the friendship of the Native Americans, the fact that illness had not claimed all their lives. Yet the purpose of the feast was not to focus on the gifts but to exalt the Giver.

Thanksgiving Today

Contemporary society has lost this most fundamental element of the Thanksgiving holiday. School children learn about friendship with the Native Americans, about good food, and about family, but God is not mentioned. Teachers and parents encourage their children to adopt an attitude of thankfulness; however, no one asks, Thankful to *whom*? *Whom* should we thank for all the blessings in our lives?

Christians need to answer this question loudly and clearly. While the culture gropes around the fringes of Thanksgiving, only believers can articulate the central message of this holiday: *Every good gift comes from God.* He provides food, safety, health, family, and friends—in addition to all the spiritual blessings belonging to those who are in Christ. Our lives are ultimately in his hands, and we are dependent on him.

This message must first be entrusted to our children. Just as thanksgiving has always been the hallmark of God's people in the past, so it should be of God's people now—during November and each day of the year.

CULTIVATING AN ATTITUDE OF GRATITUDE

I t's not fair!" complained my eight-year-old daughter. "Why do *we* have to do all the thanking? God never thanks us, but he wants us to thank him. It's just not fair!"

I inwardly groaned. *Am I not getting through to her at all?* I thought with frustration.

I was sitting on the edge of her flowered coverlet, once again try-ing to get her to say her bedtime prayers. But I wanted more than just "Now I lay me down to sleep." I wanted her to pray from her heart.

Even more important than the actual prayer, however, was the attitude. I was striving (in vain, it seemed!) to cultivate in Laura a spirit of thankfulness. It certainly didn't seem to come naturally!

For that matter, a grateful spirit does not come naturally to most of us. As Christians, we believe that all good gifts come from God. Yet thankfulness seems to be a missing ingredient in our homes today. How can we instill in our children a sense of gratitude to God and appreciation for others?

Like soil in a garden, the hearts of our children need to be culti-vated in order for gratitude to take root. I am not much of a garden-er. I like to plant flowers in May and be done with it. Weeding, hoe-ing? No thanks! My next-door neighbor, however, is a master gar-dener. His flower beds and vegetable garden are the gems of the neighborhood. How does he do it? He works at it constantly, culti-vating, planting, watering, weeding, hoeing. Every day he cares for his gardens.

We need to be just as vigilant with the hearts of our children. In big ways and in little ways, we must daily work to nurture a spirit of thankfulness.

Our Own Example

The fundamental tool for this task is our own example. Our lives speak volumes. How well we know that our children imitate us, for good or for ill! While driving through town the other day, a car cut in front of me. My son Mark blurted out, "That was a dumb thing to do! That person sure is rude!" Immediately, I recognized my own wrong attitudes and careless words coming out of the mouth of my son! Everything we are is observed by our children and reflected in their attitudes and behavior.

When I was a child, my dad and I frequently went for long walks in the woods and meadows behind our house. Dad is a real lover of beauty, a poet at heart, and frequently he quoted Robert Frost to express his wonder at God's creation. His enthusiasm was contagious. I grew up with a deep love of nature. Now I take my children for walks in the woods. Our family enjoys wilderness hiking, where together we exclaim over the grandeur of God's creation.

As parents we set the pace for expressing appreciation in the home. Mark, almost ten, has taken over the responsibility of mowing the lawn, a responsibility that used to be mine. Believe me, I express my gratitude with great enthusiasm each time he mows the lawn! Occasionally, when I know he's overburdened, I will go ahead and mow. He never fails to thank me for doing his job.

We also powerfully impress our children as we thank God for answers to prayer. Well I remember my mother's shrieks of excitement when she found a lost item for which she had prayed. "Thank you, Lord Jesus!" she would exclaim. Nothing was too trivial to bring to God in prayer, and when he answered, she openly praised him. Her enthusiastic example communicated to me that God cares about all the details of our lives and hears and answers prayer.

My most effective conversations with my children are when I simply share how God is working in my life. When my spirit is genuinely thankful, the kids seem to be, too.

Instruction

After example comes instruction, the second tool in cultivating a thankful spirit. Unfortunately, gratitude is not genetic or automatic. More than anything, thankfulness is a discipline, a good habit.

Grateful behavior in children precedes grateful attitudes. First we must teach them to show appreciation. The habit of thankfulness is learned only by practicing it, day in and day out. Then good habits of gratitude will build within children an attitude of gratitude.

Ever since my kids were little, I have insisted that they say thank you to the host or hostess when they leave someone else's house. And when a friend's mom drives them somewhere, they are to say,

"Thank you for the ride, Mrs. So-and-So." These are the simplest forms of common courtesy, yet I am continually amazed at how few children observe these basic manners. My kids usually remember to say thank you now, but it has taken years of constant reminding to establish this habit.

In addition to daily practice, special family times can reinforce lessons in gratitude. Our family uses the month of November to prepare our hearts for Thanksgiving Day using the activities and devotions mentioned in the next chapters, with many positive results.

Instruction is especially effective at teachable moments. These moments happen in the midst of the daily routine when the situation lends itself to a natural lesson in thanksgiving. We might see a tree flaming with autumn colors as we are driving. Here is an opportunity for us to express thanks for God's creativity. Or a child who had been struggling in math may come home with a math paper marked "Excellent!" What a perfect time to thank God together for helping the child understand!

Exposure

A final and very significant tool in cultivating a thankful spirit is exposure, both to those less fortunate and to other good adult role models. One Christmas, my children made homemade Christmas cards, and we brought them to patients at a nearby hospice. All of us were deeply touched as we gathered around their beds and the kids offered their own Christmas messages of comfort and hope. This exposure gave a new dimension to our Christmas celebration. We realized how blessed we are.

Another idea is to buy Christmas presents or bring Thanksgiving dinner to a needy family. For the past several years, we have purchased Christmas gifts for the five children of a single mom in inner-city Washington, D.C. After delivering the gifts to this family's small, barren row-house, we returned home with a fresh perspective on our own situation.

As our children move into the teen years, summer missions projects are great character-building opportunities. My sister spent one summer working at an orphanage on the Texas-Mexico border. Each evening the workers loaded their truck with food that the American restaurants were discarding. This was dinner for the children at a Mexican orphanage. Occasionally, the volunteers had leftovers from the orphanage. Then they drove into the Mexican village nearby and handed the food out to the impoverished inhabitants. The grateful villagers wanted to offer something in return, but all they had to offer was water. After this experience, my sister was a different person—a more grateful one.

We must be very careful to guard against indulging our children. Abundance is the biggest roadblock to a grateful spirit. Mark recently complained that some of his school friends didn't want to come to his house because he didn't have any "neat toys, like Nintendo." *If we don't have any neat toys, what are all those small items spread across our basement floor?!* I reminded him (with some indignation, I confess) that we are wealthy compared to most of the world. My children do have fewer toys and more work responsibilities than most kids we know, but they both have a wonderful imagination and are appreciative of what they receive.

Exposure to good role models can have a tremendous impact on our children. A former missionary family played a significant role in my life during my college years. The mother, Bonnie, was always brimming over with stories of God's miraculous provision in their lives. Her joyful spirit of thankfulness to God was infectious. It made me want to be like her.

Laura lay tucked under her flowered coverlet, blond curls spread out on her pillow.

"How about if I pray tonight, honey?" I suggested with a sigh of resignation.

As I thanked God for the blessings of that day, a sense of true gratitude welled up within me.

Lord, help me to cultivate the soil of her heart so that you can bring forth the blossom of a thankful spirit.

NOVEMBER FAMILY ACTIVITIES

W hat are some practical ways to help our families grow in gratitude? A positive approach is always preferable to correcting wrong behavior, nagging, or badgering. And if the positive approach is interesting and fun, all the better! Here are several suggestions for family activities during the days preceding Thanksgiving. Their purpose is simple: to remind us of all that God has done. This is an important part of being God's thankful people.

Family Reading: Stories to Make Us Thankful

In the pages that follow, you will find devotions for the ten days leading up to Thanksgiving (two years' worth, in fact). I have selected Scripture passages that highlight the wonderful ways in which God provides for us. Where space permits, I have included introductions to clarify the passage or to illustrate the theme for the day. Discussion questions, a final thought, a brief prayer, and a verse from a hymn follow the Bible reading. For a hands-on activity to help the children apply the truths to their lives, you may choose to do a Tree of Blessing or a Thanksgiving Basket.

The Tree of Blessing

The Tree of Blessing is simply a bare tree branch from your yard or park that is placed in a vase and hung with symbols of God's provision. Each of the family devotions for Thanksgiving has a corresponding symbol—a round circle with a drawing depicting something from that story.

Two to three weeks before Thanksgiving, spend a fun family evening constructing the symbols. Patterns and instructions can be found in the resource section at the back of the book. Construct the symbols ahead of time so you will be ready to hang each day's symbol on the Tree of Blessing during the ten countdown days. There is a special time to do this at the conclusion of each day's devotional.

Not only is this a fun activity that involves the entire family, but it also reinforces the Bible story. It is a visual reminder of the passage. When the children see the symbol, they remember the story and how God provided in that situation.

The Horn of Plenty

The picture of a horn overflowing with fruits and vegetables brings to mind the bounty of harvest. This traditional Thanksgiving symbol reminds us to be thankful to God for providing our food and all that we need.

Buy a horn-shaped basket, available in autumn in craft stores and grocery stores. Place this basket in a prominent position in your home. During the ten days preceding Thanksgiving, each family devotional will focus on something that God provides. Buy a variety of fruits and vegetables that will last the ten days. Small pumpkins and squashes, Indian corn, and apples are suitable. At the conclusion of each devotional, have one of the children put a fruit or vegetable into the horn of plenty. Each fruit or vegetable will represent what God provided in the Bible story and what he also provides in our lives: food, family, health, friends, and eternal life.

The Thanksgiving Basket

The Thanksgiving basket is a wonderful way to help your family count their blessings. It is a basket filled with reminders of the things for which your family is thankful. The preparation is simple. All you need is a basket, pencils, and small slips of paper.

Each devotional in the family devotions for Thanksgiving, year one, concludes with instructions for that day's addition to the Thanksgiving basket. You will be instructed to think of blessings in a particular area or category. Then you are to write down these thoughts on slips of paper. Younger children may draw pictures, tell an older family member who will write down the idea, or scribble their idea themselves. Just make sure they can provide an English translation!

As Thanksgiving approaches, the basket fills up with slips of paper, each one reminding the family of special blessings. At your Thanksgiving meal, you may want to pass the basket and have each family member draw several slips of paper. Pray around the family circle, giving thanks for the blessings that are written down on your slips of paper.

Secret Bless-Yous

(This idea is an adaptation of a Christmas idea given me by Shirley Shirock of Detroit, Michigan.)

As parents, we struggle with our children's relationships with each other. We want them to appreciate each other. This, too, is a part of Thanksgiving—being grateful and appreciative of people in our lives. In fact, the Bible teaches us that if we don't show love to the people around us, then we really don't love God (1 John 4:20).

Here's a very easy way to begin: Write down the names of your family members and put them in a hat or basket. Have family members draw a name, making sure it is not their own. Sometime the next day, family members must show appreciation in some way for their "secret buddy," the person whose name was drawn. They can make a card, collect and present several pretty leaves, or do a chore for that other family member. The idea is for each person in the family to feel blessed and appreciated by the others. But most important, this trains us all in the important habit of showing appreciation.

The Thanksgiving Book

(This idea is inspired by my friend and mentor Virginia Watson.)

Buy an ordinary composition book at the drugstore and earmark it your family's Thanksgiving book. During the two weeks prior to Thanksgiving, each evening after supper, go around the table and share three or four things for which you are especially grateful. One person should record these thoughts in your Thanksgiving book.

This proved to be a wonderful gratitude-building exercise for our family. By the time Thanksgiving rolled around, we were brimming over with gratitude for all of God's blessings in our lives.

THANKSGIVING DEVOTIONS: YEAR ONE

MONDAY

DAY 10

When we think about getting ready for Thanksgiving, we usually think about grocery lists and food preparation. This year we will be getting ready for Thanksgiving in an entirely different way. During the ten days before Thanksgiving, we will be preparing our hearts so that we learn to be thankful to God—on Thanksgiving and every day.

Specifically, we will take a look at two Old Testament prophets, Elijah and Elisha. Why? Because God provided for them and provided for others through the miracles Elijah and Elisha performed. They lived during hard times for the Israelites. The king of Israel, Ahab, was evil; he and many of the Israelites had disobeyed and ignored God, and finally God had punished the land for their disobedience.

Read—*1 Kings 17:1–6*

Now Elijah the Tishbite, from Tishbe in Gilead, said to Ahab, "As the LORD, the God of Israel, lives, whom I serve, there will be neither dew nor rain in the next few years except at my word."

Then the word of the LORD came to Elijah: "Leave here, turn eastward and hide in the Kerith Ravine, east of the Jordan. You will drink from the brook, and I have ordered the ravens to feed you there."

So he did what the LORD had told him. He went to the Kerith Ravine, east of the Jordan, and stayed there. The ravens brought him bread and meat in the morning and bread and meat in the evening, and he drank from the brook.

Discuss

1. What was the punishment for Israel's disobedience?
2. How did God provide for Elijah when he was hiding from wicked King Ahab?

3. Why do you think that God took special care of Elijah?
4. How does God provide food for you and your family?

Final Thought

Most of us have never experienced a famine. Wouldn't it be frightening not to have any food to eat? Because we have so much, we forget that without God's provision of rain and sunshine and many other things, we would not have food. This week as you pray before meals, remember to thank him, not only for the food, but for all he gives us so that we can have food (examples: rain, sun, seasons, our bodies and minds, health, energy).

Pray

Dear heavenly Father, we live because of your daily gifts to us. Thank you for our daily bread. Help those who hunger now. Amen.

Sing—*All People that on Earth Do Dwell* *(Old Hundredth)* (p. 168)

Know that the Lord is God indeed;
Without our aid he did us make.
We are his folk, he doth us feed,
And for his sheep he doth us take.

Do

Tell which foods you especially like. Write these food names on little slips of paper and place in the Thanksgiving basket. Hang the symbol of the raven on your Tree of Blessing.

Further Study for Adults

Read Psalm 23. What does this psalm say the Lord provides? Reflect on God's provision in your life, now and in the past.

TUESDAY

DAY 9

We continue to read about Elijah and the famine.

Read—*1 Kings 17:7–16*

Some time later the brook dried up because there had been no rain in the land. Then the word of the LORD came to him: "Go at once to Zarephath of Sidon and stay there. I have commanded a widow in that place to supply you with food." So he went to Zarephath. When he came to the town gate, a widow was there gathering sticks. He called to her and asked, "Would you bring me a little water in a jar so I may have a drink?" As she was going to get it, he called, "And bring me, please, a piece of bread."

"As surely as the LORD your God lives," she replied, "I don't have any bread—only a handful of flour in a jar and a little oil in a jug. I am gathering a few sticks to take home and make a meal for myself and my son, that we may eat it—and die."

Elijah said to her, "Don't be afraid. Go home and do as you have said. But first make a small cake of bread for me from what you have and bring it to me, and then make something for yourself and your son. For this is what the LORD, the God of Israel, says: 'The jar of flour will not be used up and the jug of oil will not run dry until the day the LORD gives rain on the land.'"

She went away and did as Elijah had told her. So there was food every day for Elijah and for the woman and her family. For the jar of flour was not used up and the jug of oil did not run dry, in keeping with the word of the LORD spoken by Elijah.

Discuss

1. How was the woman feeling when Elijah asked her for water?
2. What promise did Elijah give her?
3. Why do you think she was asked to make a cake for Elijah before she knew for sure that God would provide enough for her and her son?

4. Does God ever ask us to do something before we know for sure that everything will work out? Think of such a time. How did your situation turn out?

Final Thought

God gives us so many wonderful things each day simply because he loves us. Yet what he wants most of all is for us to trust him, just like children trust their earthly parents to take care of them. In order for us to know that he will take care of us, he sometimes asks us to do something scary and difficult. Then when he gives us what we need, we remember that it is God who is the giver.

Pray

Dear heavenly Father, thank you for caring for us. Thank you for faithfully keeping your promises. Amen.

Sing—*The King of Love My Shepherd Is* (p. 172)

The King of love my shepherd is,
Whose goodness faileth never;
I nothing lack if I am his
And he is mine forever.

Do

Think of a time when you trusted God and he gave you what you needed. Write this on a slip of paper and place in the Thanksgiving basket. Place the symbol of the cake and of the jar of oil on your Tree of Blessing.

Further Study for Adults

Read Romans 8:28. What are the criteria for the promise in this verse? Thank God for keeping this promise in your life.

WEDNESDAY

DAY 8

Have you ever been lost or separated from your mom or dad in a store? What did that feel like? Can you remember how happy you were to see their faces when they found you? Today's story is about the same widow we read about yesterday. In today's story, we find that the widow has lost the most important thing in the whole world to her—her son.

Read—1 Kings 17:17–24

Some time later the son of the woman who owned the house became ill. He grew worse and worse, and finally stopped breathing. She said to Elijah, "What do you have against me, man of God? Did you come to remind me of my sin and kill my son?"

"Give me your son," Elijah replied. He took him from her arms, carried him to the upper room where he was staying, and laid him on his bed. Then he cried out to the LORD, "O LORD my God, have you brought tragedy also upon this widow I am staying with, by causing her son to die?" Then he stretched himself out on the boy three times and cried to the LORD, "O LORD my God, let this boy's life return to him!"

The LORD heard Elijah's cry, and the boy's life returned to him, and he lived. Elijah picked up the child and carried him down from the room into the house. He gave him to his mother and said, "Look, your son is alive!"

Then the woman said to Elijah, "Now I know that you are a man of God and that the word of the LORD from your mouth is the truth."

Discuss

1. What happened to the boy? How did his mother feel?
2. What did Elijah do? What did God do?
3. What did the mother say when she saw her son alive again?

4. Did you know that God has given you each member of your family? And that every day that you have together is a special gift from him? When do you appreciate your family the most?

Final Thought

Showing appreciation to our family members is one way of thanking God for them. Sometimes we forget to tell family how much we love them—and what specific things about them make them special. Go around in a circle, telling what you appreciate most about the person on your right. If you want, reverse directions and do the same for the person on your left.

Pray

Dear Lord Jesus, thank you for giving us families to love us and take care of us. Help us to show love and appreciation. Amen.

Sing—*For the Beauty of the Earth* (p. 171)

For the joy of human love,
Brother, sister, parent, child,
Friends on earth and friends above;
For all gentle thoughts and mild:
Christ, our Lord, to you we raise
This our sacrifice of praise.

Do

Write down the names of family members and add these names to your basket. Hang the symbol of the boy and his mother on your Tree of Blessing.

Further Study for Adults

Read Philippians 1:3–11. For what is Paul thankful in this passage? Write the promise of verse 6 in your own words. Write Paul's prayer for the Philippians (vv. 9–11) in your own words. For whom can you claim this promise and this prayer?

THURSDAY

DAY 7

One day, Elijah and the priests of Baal, a false god, had a big competition on the top of Mount Carmel. The priests of the false god, Baal, prayed for their god to send fire from heaven onto the altar they had built for him, but nothing happened. When Elijah's turn came, he even soaked the offering and wood with water. Yet all he had to do was ask, and God sent fire from heaven. The evil queen Jezebel was furious. She sent a message to Elijah that she would have him killed within one day.

Read—1 Kings 19:3–9

Elijah was afraid and ran for his life. When he came to Beersheba in Judah, he left his servant there, while he himself went a day's journey into the desert. He came to a broom tree, sat down under it and prayed that he might die. "I have had enough, LORD," he said. "Take my life; I am no better than my ancestors." Then he lay down under the tree and fell asleep.

All at once an angel touched him and said, "Get up and eat." He looked around, and there by his head was a cake of bread baked over hot coals, and a jar of water. He ate and drank and then lay down again.

The angel of the LORD came back a second time and touched him and said, "Get up and eat, for the journey is too much for you." So he got up and ate and drank. Strengthened by that food, he traveled forty days and forty nights until he reached Horeb, the mountain of God. There he went into a cave and spent the night.

Discuss

1. What did Elijah do when he heard that Jezebel was going to kill him?
2. How was he feeling as he sat under the broom tree in the desert? What did he say that he wanted?

3. What did God give him instead?
4. Can you think of a time when you were depressed like Elijah? How did God provide for you at that time?

Final Thought

Often when we are exhausted, especially after we've done something very difficult or exciting, we become depressed. We know this is true of children, but we forget that it happens to grown-ups as well. Sometimes something else is bothering us, but first we need to make sure that our bodies have had the rest and food that they need. God uses rest, food, and good exercise to give us the strength that we need to tackle problems.

Pray

Dear Lord, thank you that each night you give us sleep to refresh us, and each day you give us food to nourish us. Amen.

Sing—*Now Thank We All Our God* (p. 175)

Oh, may this bounteous God
Through all our life be near us,
With ever joyful hearts
And blessed peace to cheer us,
And keep us in his grace,
And guide us when perplexed,
And free us from all harm
In this world and the next.

Do

Have everyone share how God helped them once when they were sad. Write these thoughts on slips of paper and add to the basket. Hang the symbol of bread and water on your Tree of Blessing.

Further Study for Adults

Read Hebrews 4. What does the writer mean by rest? How do we experience this rest?

FRIDAY

DAY 6

After Elijah spent the night in the cave, he had a personal encounter with God.

Read—*1 Kings 19:9–15, 19*

And the word of the LORD came to him: "What are you doing here, Elijah?"

He replied, "I have been very zealous for the LORD God Almighty. The Israelites have rejected your covenant, broken down your altars, and put your prophets to death with the sword. I am the only one left, and now they are trying to kill me too."

The LORD said, "Go out and stand on the mountain in the presence of the LORD, for the LORD is about to pass by."

Then a great and powerful wind tore the mountains apart and shattered the rocks before the LORD, but the LORD was not in the wind. After the wind there was an earthquake, but the LORD was not in the earthquake. After the earthquake came a fire, but the LORD was not in the fire. And after the fire came a gentle whisper. When Elijah heard it, he pulled his cloak over his face and went out and stood at the mouth of the cave.

Then a voice said to him, "What are you doing here, Elijah?"

He replied, "I have been very zealous for the LORD God Almighty. The Israelites have rejected your covenant, broken down your altars, and put your prophets to death with the sword. I am the only one left, and now they are trying to kill me too."

The LORD said to him, "Go back the way you came, and . . . anoint Elisha son of Shaphat. . . . Yet I reserve seven thousand in Israel—all whose knees have not bowed down to Baal and all whose mouths have not kissed him."

So Elijah went from there and found Elisha son of Shaphat.

Discuss

1. What happened at the mountain?

2. How did God speak to Elijah?
3. What was Elijah really upset about? What do you think Elijah needed?
4. How did God meet Elijah's need? How has God provided friends for you when you needed them?

Final Thought

Elijah thought that he was the only one left who loved the one true God. No wonder he was depressed! God knew that Elijah needed two things: He needed a new perspective and he needed a friend. God told him that there were seven thousand Israelites who still loved God, so Elijah shouldn't think that he was the last one. This gave Elijah a new perspective. Then God provided a friend and partner for Elijah, the young prophet Elisha.

Pray

Thank you, Lord Jesus, for the friends that you have given us. We especially thank you for _____ (have each family member name a special friend for whom they are thankful). Amen.

Sing—*For the Beauty of the Earth* (p. 171)

For the joy of human love,
Brother, sister, parent, child,
Friends on earth and friends above;
For all gentle thoughts and mild:
Christ, our Lord, to you we raise
This our sacrifice of praise.

Do

Write the names of friends for whom you are thankful on little slips of paper. Add these slips to your Thanksgiving basket. Hang the symbol of the mountain on your Tree of Blessing.

Further Study for Adults

Read Philippians 1:3–6. Who are your partners in the gospel? Pray a prayer of thanksgiving for your Christian friends.

SATURDAY

DAY 5

It was time for Elijah's ministry to end. Let's read about this exciting exit.

Read—*2 Kings 2:1–2, 7–14*

When the LORD was about to take Elijah up to heaven in a whirlwind, Elijah and Elisha were on their way from Gilgal. Elijah said to Elisha, "Stay here; the LORD has sent me to Bethel."

But Elisha said, "As surely as the LORD lives and as you live, I will not leave you." So they went down to Bethel.

Fifty men of the company of the prophets went and stood at a distance, facing the place where Elijah and Elisha had stopped at the Jordan. Elijah took his cloak, rolled it up and struck the water with it. The water divided to the right and to the left, and the two of them crossed over on dry ground.

When they had crossed, Elijah said to Elisha, "Tell me, what can I do for you before I am taken from you?"

"Let me inherit a double portion of your spirit," Elisha replied.

"You have asked a difficult thing," Elijah said, "yet if you see me when I am taken from you, it will be yours—otherwise not."

As they were walking along and talking together, suddenly a chariot of fire and horses of fire appeared and separated the two of them, and Elijah went up to heaven in a whirlwind. Elisha saw this and cried out, "My father! My father! The chariots and horsemen of Israel!" And Elisha saw him no more. Then he took hold of his own clothes and tore them apart.

He picked up the cloak that had fallen from Elijah and went back and stood on the bank of the Jordan. Then he took the cloak that had fallen from him and struck the water with it. "Where now is the LORD, the God of Elijah?" he asked. When he struck the water, it divided to the right and to the left, and he crossed over.

Discuss

1. How did Elisha feel about his teacher Elijah leaving him?

2. What special gift did God give to Elijah?
3. What did God give to Elisha?
4. Describe what Elisha saw and felt as Elijah was taken from him. How would you have felt if you had been there?

Final Thought

What a way to go! Most people agree that they would prefer to die in their sleep, quietly and peacefully slipping away, rather than any number of other kinds of death. But what about Elijah's exit from this world? He never had to die! That would be the best of all, wouldn't it? If we trust in Jesus Christ, God has promised that we, like Elijah, have the gift of eternal life. Our bodies may die, but the real person inside of us will live forever in happiness and peace with God.

Pray

Thank you, Father, for giving us eternal life in Christ. Amen.

Sing—*Now Thank We All Our God* (p. 175)

All praise and thanks to God
The Father now be given,
The Son, and him who reigns
With them in highest heaven,
The one eternal God,
Whom earth and heav'n adore;
For thus it was, is now,
And shall be evermore.

Do

Write down a happy thought about heaven and add this note to your Thanksgiving basket. Hang the symbol of the chariot and horses on your Tree of Blessing.

Further Study for Adults

Read Psalm 23. What does this psalm teach us about eternal life, both in this world and the next? When have you been especially thankful for God's promises of eternal life?

SUNDAY

DAY 4

Now that Elijah was gone, Elisha was God's new man for the job. God gave Elisha wisdom and power to do what he called him to do. God used Elisha to help people in need, especially people who trusted in God. During the next few days, we will see how God provided for these people through his prophet Elisha.

Read—2 Kings 4:1–7

The wife of a man from the company of the prophets cried out to Elisha, "Your servant my husband is dead, and you know that he revered the LORD. But now his creditor is coming to take my two boys as his slaves."

Elisha replied to her, "How can I help you? Tell me, what do you have in your house?"

"Your servant has nothing there at all," she said, "except a little oil."

Elisha said, "Go around and ask all your neighbors for empty jars. Don't ask for just a few. Then go inside and shut the door behind you and your sons. Pour oil into all the jars, and as each is filled, put it to one side."

She left him and afterward shut the door behind her and her sons. They brought the jars to her and she kept pouring. When all the jars were full, she said to her son, "Bring me another one."

But he replied, "There is not a jar left." Then the oil stopped flowing.

She went and told the man of God, and he said, "Go, sell the oil and pay your debts. You and your sons can live on what is left."

Discuss

1. What problem did this woman have?
2. What did she have left in her life? How do you suppose she felt?
3. How did God provide for this woman?
4. Have you ever felt like you were at the end of your rope, like you had nowhere to turn but to God? How did God help you?

Final Thought

God did not simply make a pile of money magically materialize in this woman's house. He did a tremendous miracle, and he made sure that she had more than she needed. But he required that she trust and obey. She needed to believe that Elisha was speaking for God (trust), and she needed to borrow jars and pour oil (obey). If we want to see God do amazing things, we too need to believe his Word and do what he has told us to do.

Pray

Dear Lord Jesus, thank you that you give and give to us and your goodness never runs out. Help us to trust you and obey your Word. Amen.

Sing—*The King of Love My Shepherd Is* (p. 172)

The King of love my shepherd is,
Whose goodness faileth never;
I nothing lack if I am his
And he is mine forever.

Do

Write down something that God gave to you at a time when you were in desperate need. Add this note to your Thanksgiving basket. Hang the symbol of the many jars of oil on your Tree of Blessing.

Further Study for Adults

Read Ephesians 3:20–21. How have you seen this truth manifested in your life?

MONDAY

DAY 3

For the next three days, we will read about Elisha and a woman from Shunem.

Read—2 Kings 4:8–17

One day Elisha went to Shunem. And a well-to-do woman was there, who urged him to stay for a meal. So whenever he came by, he stopped there to eat. She said to her husband, "I know that this man who often comes our way is a holy man of God. Let's make a small room on the roof and put in it a bed and a table, a chair and a lamp for him. Then he can stay there whenever he comes to us."

One day when Elisha came, he went up to his room and lay down there. He said to his servant Gehazi, "Call the Shunammite." So he called her, and she stood before him. Elisha said to him, "Tell her, 'You have gone to all this trouble for us. Now what can be done for you? Can we speak on your behalf to the king or the commander of the army?'"

She replied, "I have a home among my own people."

"What can be done for her?" Elisha asked.

Gehazi said, "Well, she has no son and her husband is old."

Then Elisha said, "Call her." So he called her, and she stood in the doorway. "About this time next year," Elisha said, "you will hold a son in your arms."

"No, my lord," she objected. "Don't mislead your servant, O man of God!" But the woman became pregnant, and the next year about that same time she gave birth to a son, just as Elisha had told her.

Discuss

1. What did the Shunammite woman do for Elisha?
2. Why do you think she wanted to do this?
3. Why did Elisha want to do something nice for the woman?
4. How did God provide for the people in this story?

Final Thought

This story shows us how generosity can be contagious! When we share with others, showing kindness, freely giving what we have to those in need, often they want to give in return. Perhaps you have a room in your house that you could share with someone who cannot afford housing. You can share by allowing someone to go in front of you in line. Even a smile and a friendly hello is a way to show Jesus' love to someone who is lonely. Don't expect anything in return. But you can be sure that good will come of it, whether you find out about the good or not!

Pray

Dear Lord, thank you for those who have been generous to me. Help me to share freely with others as well. Amen.

Sing—*For the Beauty of the Earth* (p. 171)

For the joy of human love,
Brother, sister, parent, child,
Friends on earth and friends above;
For all gentle thoughts and mild:
Christ, our Lord, to you we raise
This our sacrifice of praise.

Do

Write down a kindness for which you are thankful and add the paper to the Thanksgiving basket. Hang the symbol of the rooftop room on your Tree of Blessing.

Further Study for Adults

Read Romans 13:8–10. How did Elisha and the Shunammite woman exemplify these principles? What specific things can you do to "love your neighbor as yourself"?

TUESDAY

DAY 2

One day the Shunammite woman's son became very sick. See how God provided in this situation.

Read—2 Kings 4:18–21, 27–28, 32–37

The child grew, and one day he went out to his father, who was with the reapers.

"My head! My head!" he said to his father.

His father told a servant, "Carry him to his mother." After the servant had lifted him up and carried him to his mother, the boy sat on her lap until noon, and then he died. She went up and laid him on the bed of the man of God, then shut the door and went out.

When she reached the man of God at the mountain, she took hold of his feet. Gehazi came over to push her away, but the man of God said, "Leave her alone! She is in bitter distress, but the LORD has hidden it from me and has not told me why."

"Did I ask you for a son, my lord?" she said. "Didn't I tell you, 'Don't raise my hopes'?"

When Elisha reached the house, there was the boy lying dead on his couch. He went in, shut the door on the two of them and prayed to the LORD. Then he got on the bed and lay upon the boy, mouth to mouth, eyes to eyes, hands to hands. As he stretched himself out upon him, the boy's body grew warm. Elisha turned away and walked back and forth in the room and then got on the bed and stretched out upon him once more. The boy sneezed seven times and opened his eyes.

Elisha summoned Gehazi and said, "Call the Shunammite." And he did. When she came, he said, "Take your son." She came in, fell at his feet and bowed to the ground. Then she took her son and went out.

Discuss

1. What happened to the little boy in this story? (This was the son that Elisha promised the Shunammite woman.)
2. What did the mother do? How did she feel?

3. What can we learn from the Shunammite woman?
4. How and what did God provide in this story?

Final Thought

Have you ever received a wonderful gift only to have it snatched away from you? At times like this, we often feel angry and confused, wishing that God had never given us the gift to begin with. This woman didn't give up. She searched for God's prophet, and she asked him her hard questions. Faith isn't just sitting back and saying that everything is fine. Faith means going to God with our questions, doubts, and confusion.

Pray

Dear Lord, thank you that you love us and give us what we need, even when disappointments come. Help us to bring our problems to you and to trust that you are working for our best. Amen.

Sing—*What a Friend We Have in Jesus* (p. 180)

What a friend we have in Jesus,
All our sins and griefs to bear!
What a privilege to carry
Ev'rything to God in prayer!
Oh, what peace we often forfeit;
Oh, what needless pain we bear—
All because we do not carry
Ev'rything to God in prayer!

Do

Write down something you don't understand about God and add this slip to your Thanksgiving basket. Hang the symbol of the child on the bed on your Tree of Blessing.

Further Study for Adults

Read Deuteronomy 29:29. What are the "secret things"? What are the "things revealed"? How will this truth help you when difficulties arise?

WEDNESDAY

DAY 1

Tomorrow is Thanksgiving! Have you helped with the grocery shopping and food preparation? When we are tempted to complain about all the work, we need to remember that we are blessed to have food and a home. In today's story, we read of the Shunammite woman, who had plenty of food and a nice home until a famine came.

Read—2 Kings 8:1–6

Now Elisha had said to the woman whose son he had restored to life, "Go away with your family and stay for a while wherever you can, because the LORD has decreed a famine in the land that will last seven years." The woman proceeded to do as the man of God said. She and her family went away and stayed in the land of the Philistines seven years.

At the end of the seven years she came back from the land of the Philistines and went to the king to beg for her house and land. The king was talking to Gehazi, the servant of the man of God, and had said, "Tell me about all the great things Elisha has done." Just as Gehazi was telling the king how Elisha had restored the dead to life, the woman whose son Elisha had brought back to life came to beg the king for her house and land.

Gehazi said, "This is the woman, my lord the king, and this is her son whom Elisha restored to life." The king asked the woman about it, and she told him.

Then he assigned an official to her case and said to him, "Give back everything that belonged to her, including all the income from her land from the day she left the country until now."

Discuss

1. Why did Elisha tell the woman to move away for a while?
2. What happened when she and her family moved back to Israel?

3. These verses don't tell us exactly what happened to her house and land while she was away. What might have happened?
4. How did God provide for the Shunammite woman this time?

Final Thought

Here was an interesting "coincidence." Elisha's servant just happened to be telling the king about how Elisha raised this woman's son from the dead when in she walked! At another time, the king may not have bothered with her. But as it was, she got special attention—the royal treatment. Sometimes we forget that God is in control of this world and everything that happens in our lives. There are no coincidences. Our lives are in his hands.

Pray

Dear heavenly Father, thank you for taking care of us. You provide for all our needs. Amen.

Sing—*The King of Love My Shepherd Is* (p. 172)

The King of love my shepherd is,
Whose goodness faileth never;
I nothing lack if I am his
And he is mine forever.

Do

What does each member of your family appreciate most about your home? Add these thoughts to your Thanksgiving basket. Place the symbol of the house and land on your Tree of Blessing.

Further Study for Adults

Read 1 Peter 2:9–12. How does the passage describe the identity of God's people? What characteristics should distinguish us as a people? Why?

THANKSGIVING DEVOTIONS: YEAR TWO

MONDAY

DAY 10

When did you first realize that Jesus died to save you from your sins? Some people can point to a certain day when they prayed and asked Christ to come into their lives, and from that point on, their lives were never the same. For others of us, it was not quite so dramatic. I cannot remember a time when I did not love Jesus. From my earliest moments, my mother taught me about Jesus. I loved to go to church and worship God.

When I was seven years old, I attended vacation Bible school. One day the pastor came and talked to us about asking Jesus into our hearts. I loved Jesus already, but was he really in my heart? Silently I prayed, "Lord, just in case I haven't done this already, please come into my heart." Was that the very moment that Christ entered my life? I don't know. What I do know is this: Jesus has saved me from sin. He lives within me. And he is changing me to be more like him, little by little, day by day. Someday I will be with him in heaven, where there will be no more sin or sadness. This gift of salvation is one good reason to be very, very thankful this Thanksgiving—and always.

Read—*Ephesians 2:8–9*

For it is by grace you have been saved, through faith—and this not from yourselves, it is the gift of God—not by works, so that no one can boast.

Discuss

1. What is a gift?
2. What gift do these verses talk about?
3. How is receiving a gift different from getting paid for a job?
4. Sometimes we think that if we are good, God will love us more. What do these verses tell us about that idea?

Final Thought

Grace is what God shows us when we deserve to be punished but God gives us presents instead. God loves to show us his grace. We don't deserve the gift of salvation. What we really deserve is the cross. But Jesus took our punishment for us so that we could have all the blessings of heaven. Have you ever accepted this wonderful gift of salvation? If not, how about accepting it right now?

Pray

Lord Jesus Christ, thank you for taking my punishment and dying on the cross for me. I accept your gift of salvation. Amen.

Sing—*The King of Love My Shepherd Is* (p. 172)

The King of love my shepherd is,
Whose goodness faileth never;
I nothing lack if I am his
And he is mine forever.

Perverse and foolish oft I strayed,
But yet in love he sought me,
And on his shoulder gently laid,
And home, rejoicing brought me.

Do

Hang the symbol of the cross on your Tree of Blessing.

Further Study for Adults

Read Romans 8:31–39. What does this passage teach us about God's grace? Write a prayer of thanksgiving for these blessings in your life.

TUESDAY

DAY 9

How do you feel when you know that you have done something very wrong? Several years ago, my friend Leslie told me a secret. She didn't say, "Don't tell anyone. It's a secret." But even though she didn't say it was a secret, I knew it was a secret anyway. What do you think I did? I told someone else Leslie's secret. Later on I was talking to Leslie on the phone. She could tell from the things I was saying that I was not telling her my own thoughts. They were thoughts that had come from someone else.

"Ann, you didn't tell anyone my secret, did you?" she asked. I felt my face turn very hot. I could not lie to my friend. "Yes, I did," I had to admit. I felt ashamed.

Leslie could have said, "Well, I will never tell you another secret as long as I live. I can't trust you anymore." But she didn't. She forgave me, even though I had hurt and disappointed her. I didn't deserve it, but she forgave me. When we come to know Christ, he forgives our sins.

Read—*Colossians 2:13–14*

When you were dead in your sins . . . God made you alive with Christ. He forgave us all our sins, having canceled the written code, with its regulations, that was against us and that stood opposed to us; he took it away, nailing it to the cross.

Discuss

1. Can you think of some things that you have done that made God unhappy? What about things you did today?
2. When we sin, does it make us happy or unhappy?
3. What does God want us to do after we sin?
4. What does it mean that he will make us alive with Christ?

Final Thought

The written code (the law that God gave to Moses) said that we had to keep all of God's law or we would die. No one but Jesus could ever do that! That code was nailed to the cross with Jesus! Because of the cross, God is able to forgive us for all our sins. Nothing we can do is too bad for God to forgive. Let's thank God for the gift of forgiveness.

Pray

Dear Lord Jesus, we do things every day that make you unhappy. We are so sorry. Thank you for forgiving us. Amen.

Sing—*Praise, My Soul, the King of Heaven* (p. 179)

Praise, my soul, the King of heaven;
To his feet your tribute bring.
Ransomed, healed, restored, forgiven,
Evermore his praises sing.
Alleluia! Alleluia!
Praise the everlasting King!

Do

Hang the symbol of the tablets on your Tree of Blessing.

Further Study for Adults

Read Luke 15:11–32. What does this parable teach us about God's grace and forgiveness? Contrast the responses of the two sons. To which son can you best relate? What recent experiences qualify you as a prodigal? Reflect on God's forgiveness in your life.

WEDNESDAY

DAY 8

Another gift that God gives us with the gift of salvation is the gift of eternal life. That means two things. First, it means that even now, here on earth, we begin to live a new and better life. But it also means that when our bodies die, we will live forever with Jesus.

Have you ever had a loved one die? When I was in third grade, my grandfather died. Grandpa had lived with us all my life until he got sick a year before his death.

Grandpa had a stroke and, after some time in the hospital, was moved to a nearby nursing home. Mom visited him every day. Sometimes I went along. It was strange to see my old buddy lying in a bed with tubes coming out of his nose. Then one day Mom told me that Grandpa had gone to be with the Lord.

I went to the funeral, and there was Grandpa, lying in the long silver box. But I knew that that wasn't really Grandpa. His body was there, but Grandpa was in heaven.

When Jesus was thinking about his own upcoming death, he talked to his disciples about heaven. He gave them, and us, a very special promise.

Read—*John 14:1–3*

Do not let your hearts be troubled. Trust in God; trust also in me. In my Father's house are many rooms; if it were not so, I would have told you. I am going there to prepare a place for you. And if I go and prepare a place for you, I will come back and take you to be with me that you also may be where I am.

Discuss

1. What do you think heaven will be like?
2. Who do we know will be there with us?
3. How do Jesus' words help us when we think about death?

4. What difference does this make in how we live out our lives here on earth?

Final Thought

When someone we love dies, it is right for us to feel sad. We will miss that person. Our lives will never be the same. But if our loved one believed in Jesus, we know that he or she is in a wonderful place. Jesus tells us that in heaven, he will wipe away every tear. Nothing bad ever happens there. No one is mean. No one gets hurt. And we get to be with Jesus himself! He loves us completely and perfectly!

Pray

Dear Lord Jesus, thank you for preparing a place for us in heaven. Thank you for the gift of eternal life. Amen.

Sing—*The King of Love My Shepherd Is* (p. 172)

And so, through all the length of days,
Thy goodness faileth never.
Good Shepherd, may I sing thy praise
Within thy house forever.

Do

Hang the symbol of the house on your Tree of Blessing.

Further Study for Adults

Read 2 Peter 3:8–14. What will the Day of the Lord be like? How is heaven described? According to verse 14, what impact should this hope have on our lifestyle? Reflect on the gift of eternal life. How is this gift making a difference in your life?

THURSDAY

DAY 7

Do you know anyone who was adopted as a baby? If you love Jesus, you are adopted by God into his family. That is a very special privilege. Our friends the Springs were not able to have children the way most parents do, so they decided to try to adopt a baby. They waited for many long months.

One day the adoption agency called and told them about a baby boy in Korea who needed two loving parents. Beth and Jeff were so excited as they showed us his picture and tried to pronounce his long Korean name. But he was still too young to make the long trip halfway around the world. Our friends had to wait even longer.

At long last, the call came telling them that their baby was on his way. They ran out and bought diapers and baby formula. It was the day before Thanksgiving when Jonathan arrived. Beth and Jeff were at the airport, waiting with pounding hearts, when the person who had held Jonathan for twenty-one hours appeared at the gate with him in her arms. That evening the Springs walked into the Thanksgiving eve church service carrying their new son. The congregation burst into applause!

Read—*Ephesians 1:4–6*

For he chose us in him before the creation of the world to be holy and blameless in his sight. In love he predestined us to be adopted as his sons through Jesus Christ, in accordance with his pleasure and will—to the praise of his glorious grace, which he has freely given us in the One he loves.

Discuss

1. What is so special about being adopted?
2. What kind of a father is God? How does he treat his children?
3. When did God choose us and why?

4. How should we respond to God as we think about the gift of adoption into his family?

Final Thought

Our friends had very thankful hearts that night as they held their precious son. And we rejoiced with them. Jesus told us that there is great rejoicing in heaven over every sinner who repents (Luke 15:7). That means that every time someone is adopted into God's heavenly family, all the angels clap and celebrate! Aren't you glad that your heavenly Father chose you and adopted you?

Pray

Dear heavenly Father, we don't understand it, but we are so thankful that you have adopted us as your children. Amen.

Sing—*The King of Love My Shepherd Is* (p. 172)

The King of love my shepherd is,
Whose goodness faileth never;
I nothing lack if I am his
And he is mine forever.

Do

Hang the symbol of the baby on your Tree of Blessing.

Further Study for Adults

Read John 1:12–13 and Romans 8:14–17. What do these verses tell us about sonship? As fellow heirs with Christ, what do we share with him? How can this help us to be thankful in the midst of difficulties? Write a thank you letter to your heavenly Father for your inheritance as his adoptive child.

FRIDAY

DAY 6

Corrie ten Boom was a young woman living in the Netherlands with her sister Betsy and their father at the time that the Nazis invaded. The Nazis wanted to get rid of all Jewish people. The ten Booms loved God, so they hid Jews in their home and helped them to get out of the country.

One day they were caught. Corrie, Betsy, and their father were sent to a terrible place called a concentration camp. There the Nazis beat, tortured, and killed the prisoners. Corrie's father died. Betsy and Corrie clung to God's promises and inspired many other prisoners, even as they all suffered terribly. Finally Betsy also died. Then one day, through a mistake in some paperwork, Corrie was released.

Many years after the war, Corrie was speaking to a large group about the love of God. After her talk, a man came up to her and wanted to shake her hand. He said that he had been a Nazi guard at her prison camp. Jesus had forgiven his sins and given him a new life. Corrie recognized him as the cruelest guard in the camp. A feeling, a hatred welled up inside her. Silently she asked God to help her to forgive this man. The Lord helped her to put out her hand. As she did, a feeling like an electric shock surged through her body and love filled her heart—love that came from God.

Read—*1 John 3:16*

This is how we know what love is: Jesus Christ laid down his life for us. And we ought to lay down our lives for our brothers.

Discuss

1. Can you think of someone you have a hard time loving?
2. What does Jesus want you to do about this?
3. How did God demonstrate his love for us?
4. Discuss what it means to "lay down our lives for our brothers." Think of some specific things you can do to love those difficult

people as verse eighteen of the same passage says, "with actions and in truth."

Final Thought

When I have a hard time loving someone, I have learned, like Corrie, to pray, asking God to fill me with his love. I also pray for that person, that God's best will work out in his or her life. Then I try to do something kind for that person. Perhaps it is a smile, a phone call, a friendly card, or a pan of brownies I give that person. God's love begins to work in my heart—and in the other person's, too. We might not end up best friends, but the important thing is that I be obedient to God. I need to leave the outcome to him.

Pray

Dear Lord Jesus, thank you for showing us the greatest love there is by laying down your life. Fill us with your love. Amen.

Sing—*Come Down, O Love Divine* (p. 170)

Come down, O Love divine;
Seek thou this soul of mine
And visit it with thine own ardor glowing;
O Comforter, draw near;
Within my heart appear
And kindle it, thy holy flame bestowing.

Do

Hang the symbol of the open prison door on your Tree of Blessing.

Further Study for Adults

Read Matthew 5:43–48. According to Jesus, what does our Father require of us? Why? Who are your enemies? What steps can you take today to begin to love them?

SATURDAY

DAY 5

Isn't it hard to be good all the time? Well, guess what? It's not just hard—it's impossible! We all struggle with being good, no matter how old or young we are, no matter how long we have been Christians. As long as we are living on this earth, sin is still very much a part of us.

Just a few weeks ago, Laura felt frustrated when she had disobeyed me. She collapsed on my bed in a heap. "I'll never change, Mom. You'll just have to get used to me the way I am. I've prayed about it, and it seems like God isn't listening. There just isn't any hope for me."

I put my arm around her and assured her that I had seen a lot of wonderful changes in her. God was at work, even though sometimes it didn't feel like it.

I too struggle with the same sins over and over again. But I can look back and see that God has changed me in very specific ways. And that's a miracle!

God has promised to give us the strength to obey him. Power to do what is right is a great gift that God has given those who love him.

Read—2 Peter 1:3

His divine power has given us everything we need for life and godliness through our knowledge of him who called us by his own glory and goodness.

Discuss

1. What has God's power given us?
2. Can you think of some recent situations in which you have needed God's divine power?
3. How do we get this power?
4. What steps can you take today to begin to realize God's power in your life?

Final Thought

This power is ours, not because of anything we have done, but because of God's glory and goodness. As we get to know God better—by reading his Word, praying, and worshiping him—his power begins to work in our hearts. He makes us want to do what is right. Then he gives us the strength to do it. So even when we are good, it is all because of Jesus!

Pray

Dear Lord Jesus, thank you for your power that is working inside me to change me and make me more like you. Amen.

Sing—*The King of Love My Shepherd Is* (p. 172)

Perverse and foolish oft I strayed,
But yet in love he sought me,
And on his shoulder gently laid,
And home, rejoicing brought me.

Do

Hang on your Tree of Blessing the symbol of the shepherd carrying the lamb on his shoulders.

Further Study for Adults

Read 2 Peter 1:3–11. How can we participate in the divine nature and escape corruption? What qualities are we to work toward? What are some specific steps you can take today and in the coming week to begin to possess some of these qualities?

SUNDAY

DAY 4

Do you ever get worried? Most of us do. But God doesn't want us to feel worried and afraid. Several days ago, Laura was terribly worried about a big test. Her teacher had talked about the importance of this test for the past several months, and the next day was the first day of the test. Laura was beside herself with worry.

As I tucked her into bed, we talked about the test and Laura's fears. I assured her that she would do just fine. And even if she didn't, it wouldn't be the end of the world. But my words did little to take away her fears. Then I prayed for her. She seemed comforted by my prayer. With a kiss, I turned out the light and said good-night.

A few minutes later I heard a knock at my bedroom door. "I think I need to pray one more time," said Laura. She prayed this time, and as she said good-night, I could see that God had given her his peace. The next morning, before Laura headed for the bus stop, she reminded me to pray for her.

I couldn't wait to hear how the test had gone. Sure enough, Laura felt that she had done very well. Our prayers were full of thanksgiving that evening.

Read—Philippians 4:6–7

Do not be anxious about anything, but in everything, by prayer and petition, with thanksgiving, present your requests to God. And the peace of God, which transcends all understanding, will guard your hearts and your minds in Christ Jesus.

Discuss

1. What aren't we supposed to worry about?
2. Instead of worrying, what does God want us to do?
3. What will happen when we pray about our problems?

4. Can you think of some things that are worrying you right now? Ask your family to pray with you about these concerns. (Note: Be sure not to give advice. Just pray!)

Final Thought

Three words in these verses catch my attention: *anything, everything,* and *all.* These words remind us that we have a big God. Nothing is too little or too big for him. God cares about all our concerns. We don't need to worry, because our lives are in the hands of a great and mighty God who loves us.

Pray

Dear heavenly Father, thank you for hearing and answering our prayers and for giving us your peace. Amen.

Sing—*What a Friend We Have in Jesus* (p. 180)

What a friend we have in Jesus,
All our sins and griefs to bear!
What a privilege to carry
Ev'rything to God in prayer!
Oh, what peace we often forfeit;
Oh, what needless pain we bear—
All because we do not carry
Ev'rything to God in prayer!

Do

Hang the symbol of the praying hands on your Tree of Blessing.

Further Study for Adults

Read John 14:25–27. With what does Jesus associate the gift of his peace? According to these verses, what action does the Holy Spirit take in our lives? How is this a means of receiving God's peace? Can you think of instances in your own life when the Holy Spirit brought you peace through God's Word? Pray now, giving thanks for the "peace which passes all understanding."

MONDAY

DAY 3

One of the best gifts God gives us is the gift of his Holy Spirit.

Read—*Acts 8:26–31, 35–39*

Now an angel of the Lord said to Philip, "Go south to the road—the desert road—that goes down from Jerusalem to Gaza." So he started out, and on his way he met an Ethiopian eunuch, an important official in charge of all the treasury of Candace, queen of the Ethiopians. This man had gone to Jerusalem to worship, and on his way home was sitting in his chariot reading the book of Isaiah the prophet. The Spirit told Philip, "Go to that chariot and stay near it."

Then Philip ran up to the chariot and heard the man reading Isaiah the prophet. "Do you understand what you are reading?" Philip asked.

"How can I," he said, "unless someone explains it to me?" So he invited Philip to come up and sit with him.

Then Philip began with that very passage of Scripture and told him the good news about Jesus.

As they traveled along the road, they came to some water and the eunuch said, "Look, here is some water. Why shouldn't I be baptized?" And he gave orders to stop the chariot. Then both Philip and the eunuch went down into the water and Philip baptized him. When they came up out of the water, the Spirit of the Lord suddenly took Philip away, and the eunuch did not see him again, but went on his way rejoicing.

Discuss

1. What did the Spirit tell Philip to do?
2. Why do you suppose the Spirit led Philip to this officer?
3. What does this incident show us about how God works?
4. Can you think of any time in your life when you knew that the Spirit was leading you?

Final Thought

You may not hear a real voice when the Holy Spirit leads you. Often we are not even aware of the Spirit's leading and only later do we realize that the Spirit must have led us to a certain place or a certain person. If you have asked Jesus to come into your heart, the Holy Spirit is in you. That gift is yours, now and forever. But day by day, we need to keep our eyes, ears, and hearts open. If we desire to please him and live for him, the Holy Spirit will be free to lead us, just as he did Philip.

Pray

Dear Father, thank you for the gift of your Holy Spirit. Give us open, seeking hearts to follow your leading. Amen.

Sing—*Come Down, O Love Divine* (p. 170)

Come down, O Love divine;
Seek thou this soul of mine
And visit it with thine own ardor glowing;
O Comforter, draw near;
Within my heart appear
And kindle it, thy holy flame bestowing.

Do

Hang the symbol of the Bible and flame on your Tree of Blessing.

Further Study for Adults

Read John 16:5–15. What do these verses teach us about the work of the Holy Spirit? Reflect on his work in your life. What steps can you take today to make yourself more available to him? Thank God for his presence in your life and the difference that he makes.

TUESDAY

DAY 2

My friend Linda had just given her life to Christ when I met her in a small Sunday school class. There were only four of us in the class. Each Sunday morning the class studied the Bible together, but Linda did not have one Christian friend. One day, desperate, she privately prayed that God would bring a Christian friend to her. I had no idea that Linda prayed this, yet later that very day, I asked Linda if she would like to get together once a week and study the Bible. Her eyes widened and in a startled voice she replied, "Why, yes! I'd really like that a lot!"

Over the next five years, Linda and I met regularly to study the Bible and pray. Our friendship turned out to be the answer to Linda's prayer. God used each of us in the other's life.

As a brand-new Christian, Linda had several things in her life that "Christians don't do." While I knew about these things, God amazingly kept my mouth shut. It was as if he said, *Don't worry, Ann. As Linda gets to know me better, I will take care of those things one by one. You just help her get to know me.* And that is exactly what happened! It wasn't long before Linda's life became an example to me! She continues to inspire me and spur me on to love and obey Jesus.

We come to know God when we accept Christ. As we get to know him better, we become more like him. Only this can make us truly happy.

Read—*John 17:3*

Now this is eternal life: that they may know you, the only true God, and Jesus Christ, whom you have sent.

Discuss

1. This verse is from a prayer that Jesus prayed to his heavenly Father. What does he say is eternal life?
2. What do these verses tell us about God?

3. How are we able to know God?

4. How are you seeking to know God better?

Final Thought

It is so easy to get lazy in our Christian life. Reading the Bible and praying are so much work! And really growing through faith and obedience is even harder! Yet only as we come to know God better can we really become the people God wants us to be. And it brings us so much joy! We wonder why we dreaded it when we find that knowing Christ is more wonderful than anything else on earth!

Pray

Dear Lord Jesus Christ, thank you for letting us come to know you. Thank you that knowing you changes us. Amen.

Sing—*Now Thank We All Our God* (p. 175)

Oh, may this bounteous God
Through all our life be near us,
With ever joyful hearts
And blessed peace to cheer us,
And keep us in his grace,
And guide us when perplexed,
And free us from all harm
In this world and the next.

Do

Hang the symbol of the Bible on your Tree of Blessing.

Further Study for Adults

Read Philippians 3:7–11. Write these verses out in your own words. Which of Paul's sentiments reflect your own thoughts? Which do you find difficult to understand? Why would Paul want to know (experience) the fellowship of sharing in Christ's sufferings? Write a prayer that expresses your desire to know Christ better.

WEDNESDAY

DAY 1

For several years our living room stood empty, used only as a tumbling room for the kids. When the time came to furnish it, we decided to try to buy as much secondhand furniture as we could. Every Friday I scoured the classifieds under "Furniture." Many Fridays and Saturdays I scouted out estate sales.

The first piece I found was a lovely oval-shaped mahogany coffee table, very unusual in its design. My next project was to find two side tables. Imagine my amazement when I entered an estate sale and saw two end tables that matched our new coffee table! My final and most exciting adventure involved a long, narrow table that I found through the classifieds. It didn't quite fit into my car. The back door of the station wagon had to be tied down after I set the extensions and drawers in the back with the table. As I turned onto a busy street, the extensions flew out the back of my car. I pulled over to the side, jumped out, and watched as several cars ran over them.

"No!" I cried and plunged into the street. At that very moment, a car whizzed by, missing me by only a few inches. I looked both ways the next time and ran out, rescued my table extensions, and tucked them in the front seat. The Lord not only provided a beautiful table for me, but he also saved my life despite my foolishness. And the table extensions were barely scratched!

Read—*Philippians 4:19*

And my God will meet all your needs according to his glorious riches in Christ Jesus.

Discuss

1. Can you think of a time when God met your needs?
2. How many of our needs will God meet?
3. What is the difference between wants and needs?

4. According to this verse, how is God able to meet our needs? What does this mean?

Final Thought

My furniture adventures perhaps seem silly, especially when so much of our world is in need of the basics: food, shelter, clothing. Yet if we learn to look to God for the little things day by day, then when we find ourselves in great need, we will know how to trust him. Every good gift comes from God (see James 1:17). This Thanksgiving, let's look around at all that he has given us—and be thankful!

Pray

Dear heavenly Father, we thank you for taking such good care of us and providing for all our needs through Jesus Christ. Amen.

Sing—*Now Thank We All Our God* (p. 175)

Now thank we all our God
With hearts and hands and voices,
Who wondrous things has done,
In whom his world rejoices;
Who, from our mothers' arms,
Has blest us on our way
With countless gifts of love,
And still is ours today.

Do

Hang the symbol of the table on your Tree of Blessing.

Further Study for Adults

Read Romans 8:32. Write this verse in your own words. Read the rest of the chapter to determine the context. What do you suppose Paul means by "how will he not also, along with him, graciously give us all things"? Reflect on some of the things, along with Christ, that God has given us.

THANKSGIVING FAMILY CELEBRATION

A merican tradition dictates that the turkey be the centerpiece of the Thanksgiving celebration. The delicious festive meal, shared with family and friends, deserves a place of prominence on this beloved holiday.

The food itself, however, should not eclipse the God who provided it. This can easily happen. Preparation for Thanksgiving dinner and clean-up afterwards are quite a production. It is difficult to have your mind on spiritual things and at the same time keep track of when the turkey comes out of the oven and how to keep your gravy from having lumps in it. For that reason, someone other than the cook must be responsible for the spiritual dimension of Thanksgiving.

Here are several suggestions for making your Thanksgiving Day celebration a spiritual event in which the family focuses with thankful hearts on God's great goodness. First are some ideas for the prayer and the mealtime conversation. Then there is a model for an after-dinner time of family worship.

The Thanksgiving Meal

The Prayer

Before the meal, have one of the children pass out pencils and small slips of paper, three slips of paper for each person present. Instruct everyone to think of three things for which he or she is especially thankful. These things should be as specific and brief as possible. Write these three things on the three slips of paper. (Preschoolers may draw a picture of each thing for which they are thankful.) Everyone should bring the slips of paper to the table when dinner is served.

The leader—the person responsible for the spiritual elements of the celebration—should have a basket at his or her place at the table. This may be the same basket that the family used during the pre-Thanksgiving devotions. If so, it already has a number of slips of paper in it.

Starting with the person to the right of the leader, go around the table, each person offering thanks to God for the three things that they have written on their slips of paper. Pass the basket at the same time, so that the basket is always in front of the person who is giving thanks. After that person gives thanks, he or she places the three slips of paper in the basket and passes the basket on to the next person. Continue around the circle until the basket is once again in front of the leader. After the leader gives thanks for his or her three specific things and places the three slips of paper in the basket, he or she lifts the basket up and offers a prayer of general thanksgiving.

This activity is like taking an offering in church, except that this is an offering of thanks. God desires our thanks every bit as much as our money. The writer to the Hebrews instructs us, "Through Jesus, therefore, let us continually offer to God a sacrifice of praise—the fruit of lips that confess his name" (Heb. 13:15).

The Conversation

During the meal, let your conversation dwell on God's goodness to your family in the past year. Encourage each person to share one way in which God has helped him or her during the past twelve months. This input will provide the basis for your Litany of Thanksgiving that is described in the next section.

Family Worship on Thanksgiving Day

Call to Worship

Leader: Praise the Lord. Give thanks to the Lord, for he is good.

All: His love endures forever.

Read—1 Chronicles 29:10–13

Praise be to you, O LORD,
    God of our father Israel,
    from everlasting to everlasting.
Yours, O LORD, is the greatness and the power
    and the glory and the majesty and the splendor,
    for everything in heaven and earth is yours.
Yours, O LORD, is the kingdom;
    you are exalted as head over all.
Wealth and honor come from you;

you are the ruler of all things.
In your hands are strength and power
   to exalt and give strength to all.
Now, our God, we give you thanks,
   and praise your glorious name.

Sing—*All People That on Earth Do Dwell (Old Hundredth)* (p. 168)

All people that on earth do dwell,
Sing to the Lord with cheerful voice;
Him serve with mirth, his praise forth tell,
Come ye before him, and rejoice.

Know that the Lord is God indeed;
Without our aid he did us make.
We are his folk, he doth us feed,
And for his sheep he doth us take.

Oh, enter then his gates with praise;
Approach with joy his courts unto;
Praise, laud, and bless his name always,
For it is seemly so to do.

For why? The Lord our God is good:
His mercy is for ever sure;
His truth at all times firmly stood,
And shall from age to age endure.

To Father, Son, and Holy Ghost,
The God whom heaven and earth adore,
From men and from the angel-host
Be praise and glory evermore. Amen.

Litany of Thanksgiving

Write a family psalm of thanksgiving based on God's faithfulness and provision in the past. This psalm can be written during dinner or discussed during dinner and written down afterward. Think together as a family about your past and how God has provided for you in specific situations. Write down how God helped you in each of these circumstances, using short, psalm-like sentences interspersed with the refrain, "Your love endures forever." As a model, see Psalm 136. Recite your family psalm at this point in your family worship celebration on Thanksgiving. Each person takes a turn reading a line and the rest of the family joins in the refrain.

You may want to have one of the children copy your family psalm neatly on a sheet of white paper and glue it to colorful construction paper or posterboard. Then post it somewhere as a constant reminder to your family to be thankful for God's work in your lives.

Sing—*Now Thank We All Our God* (p. 175)

Now thank we all our God
With heart and hands and voices,
Who wondrous things has done,
In whom his world rejoices;
Who, from our mothers' arms,
Has blessed us on our way
With countless gifts of love,
And still is ours today.

Oh, may this bounteous God
Through all our life be near us,
With ever joyful hearts
And blessed peace to cheer us;
And keep us in his grace,
And guide us when perplexed,
And free us from all harm
In this world and the next.

All praise and thanks to God
The Father now be given,
The Son, and him who reigns
With them in highest heaven,
The one eternal God,
Whom earth and heaven adore;

For thus it was, is now,
And shall be evermore.

Close of Worship

Leader: Praise be to the Lord, the God of Israel, from everlasting to
everlasting. Let all the people say:

All: Amen! Praise the Lord!

INSTRUCTIONS:
TREE OF SAINTS
AND TREE OF BLESSING

Materials

- One tree branch (lightweight, but with lots of small branches)
- One pot or vase for holding tree branch
- Soil or rocks for weighting down pot or vase
- Posterboard in red, orange, and/or yellow
- Crayons or washable markers
- Scissors
- Glue or gluestick
- Paper punch
- Yarn, string, or metal ornament hooks

Making the Tree

1. Set tree branch in pot or vase. Support the tree branch by filling the vase or pot with soil or rocks. This will be the holiday tree itself.
2. Photocopy the symbols for the holiday tree on pp. 146–65 of this book.
3. Color the symbols, using crayons, markers, paints—whatever medium you chose. The entire family can participate.
4. Cut out the circles. Even small children can help as long as they have blunt-end scissors.
5. Using one of the circles as a pattern, draw 24 circles on the piece of posterboard. Adults or older children will have to cut out these circles.
6. Glue the paper circles with the colored symbols onto the poster-board circle backings. This is fun and easy for the small ones to do, especially if they have gluesticks.
7. On the posterboard backing, write the day number and the Scripture verse or the story that correspond to each symbol.
8. Optional: At this point, you may want to bring your circles to a print shop and have them laminated. This is an inexpensive way to ensure that the circles last for years to come.
9. Punch a hole in the top of each circle, about 1/4 inch from the top edge.

10. Cut 24 lengths of yarn or string. Each length should be about 10 to 12 inches. (Optional: simply use ornament hooks, which you can buy inexpensively at the drugstore. Yarn is safer to use with small children, however.)
11. Tie strings through holes in circles.

To Use the Holiday Tree

1. Keep the circles (symbols) in a manila envelope or a resealable plastic bag.
2. Before each devotional time, find the symbol that is indicated for that day's reading.
3. At the conclusion of the family devotions, allow a child to place the symbol on the tree. You may have to hang several symbols on each branch.

SYMBOL PATTERNS

HYMNS

All People that on Earth Do Dwell (Old Hundredth)

1 All peo - ple that on earth do dwell, Sing to the
2 Know that the Lord is God in - deed; With - out our
3 Oh, en - ter then his gates with praise; Ap - proach with
4 For why? The Lord our God is good: His mer - cy

Lord with cheer - ful voice; Him serve with mirth, his
aid he did us make. We are his folk, he
joy his courts un - to; Praise, laud, and bless his
is for - ev - er sure; His truth at all times

praise forth tell; Come ye be - fore him and re - joice.
doth us feed, And for his sheep he doth us take.
name al - ways, For it is seem - ly so to do.
firm - ly stood, And shall from age to age en - dure.

5 To Father, Son, and Holy Ghost,
   The God whom heav'n and earth adore,
   From us and from the angel host
   Be praise and glory evermore.

The Church's One Foundation

169

Come Down, O Love Divine

For the Beauty of the Earth

1 For the beau - ty of the earth, For the beau - ty of the skies,
2 For the won - der of each hour Of the day and of the night,
3 For the joy of ear and eye, For the heart and mind's de - light,
4 For the joy of hu - man love, Broth-er, sis - ter, par - ent, child,

For the love which from our birth O - ver and a - round us lies:
Hill and vale and tree and flow'r, Sun and moon and stars of light:
For the mys - tic har - mo - ny Link-ing sense to sound and sight:
Friends on earth and friends a - bove; For all gen - tle thoughts and mild:

Refrain

Christ, our Lord, to you we raise This our sac - ri - fice of praise.

171

The King of Love My Shepherd Is

1 The King of love my shep-herd is, Whose good - ness fail - eth nev - er; I noth - ing lack if I am his And he is mine for - ev - er.

2 Where streams of liv - ing wa - ter flow, My ran - somed soul he lead - eth And, where the ver - dant pas - tures grow, With food ce - les - tial feed - eth.

3 Per - verse and fool - ish oft I strayed, But yet in love he sought me, And on his shoul - der gent - ly laid, And home, re - joic - ing, brought me.

4 In death's dark vale I fear no ill, With thee, dear Lord, be - side me, Thy rod and staff my com - fort still; Thy cross be - fore to guide me.

Love Divine, All Loves Excelling

1 Love di-vine, all loves ex-cel-ling, Joy of heav'n, to earth come
2 Breathe, oh, breathe thy lov-ing Spir-it In-to ev-'ry trou-bled
3 Come, Al-might-y, to de-liv-er; Let us all thy life re-
4 Fin-ish then thy new cre-a-tion, Pure and spot-less let us

down! Fix in us thy hum-ble dwell-ing, All thy faith-ful
breast; Let us all in thee in-her-it; Let us find thy
ceive; Sud-den-ly re-turn, and nev-er, Nev-er-more thy
be; Let us see thy great sal-va-tion Per-fect-ly re-

mer-cies crown. Je-sus, thou art all com-pas-sion,
prom-ised rest. Take a-way the love of sin-ning;
tem-ples leave. Thee we would be al-ways bless-ing,
stored in thee! Changed from glo-ry in-to glo-ry,

Pure, un-bound-ed love thou art; Vis-it us with
Al-pha and O-me-ga be; End of faith, as
Serve thee as thy hosts a-bove, Pray, and praise thee
Till in heav'n we take our place, Till we cast our

thy sal - va - tion, En - ter ev - 'ry trem - bling heart.
its be - gin - ning, Set our hearts at lib - er - ty.
with - out ceas - ing, Glo - ry in thy per - fect love.
crowns be - fore thee, Lost in won - der, love, and praise!

My Faith Looks Up to Thee

1 My faith looks up to thee, Thou Lamb of Cal - va - ry,
2 May thy rich grace im - part Strength to my faint - ing heart,
3 While life's dark maze I tread And griefs a - round me spread,
4 When ends life's tran - sient dream, When death's cold, sul - len stream

Sav - ior di - vine! Now hear me while I pray, Take all my
My zeal in - spire; As thou hast died for me, Oh, may my
Be thou my guide; Bid dark - ness turn to day, Wipe sor - row's
Shall o'er me roll; Blest Sav - ior, then, in love Fear and dis -

guilt a - way, Oh, let me from this day Be whol - ly thine!
love to thee Pure, warm, and change - less be, A liv - ing fire!
tears a - way, Nor let me ev - er stray From thee a - side.
trust re - move; Oh, bear me safe a - bove, A ran - somed soul!

174

Now Thank We All Our God

O Jesus, I Have Promised

1 O Je - sus, I have prom - ised To serve you to the end;
2 Oh, let me feel you near me; The world is ev - er near.
3 Oh, let me hear you speak - ing In ac - cents clear and still
4 O Je - sus, you have prom - ised To all who fol - low you

Re - main for - ev - er near me, My mas - ter and my friend.
I see the sights that daz - zle, The tempt - ing sounds I hear.
A - bove the storms of pas - sion, The mur - murs of self - will.
That where you are in glo - ry Your ser - vant shall be too.

I shall not fear the bat - tle If you are by my side,
My foes are ev - er near me, A - round me and with - in;
Now speak to re - as - sure me, To has - ten or con - trol;
And Je - sus, I have prom - ised To serve you to the end;

Nor wan - der from the path - way If you will be my guide.
But, Je - sus, then draw near - er To shield my soul from sin.
Now speak and make me lis - ten, O Guard - ian of my soul.
Oh, give me grace to fol - low, My mas - ter and my friend.

O Word of God Incarnate

O Zion, Haste

1 O Zi - on, haste, your mis - sion high ful - fill - ing,
2 Pub - lish to ev - 'ry peo - ple, tongue, and na - tion
3 Give of your own to bear the mes - sage glo - rious,
4 He comes a - gain! O Zi - on, ere you meet him,

To tell to all the world that God is light; That he who
That God, in whom they live and move, is love; Tell how he
Give of your wealth to speed them on their way, Pour out your
Make known to ev - 'ry heart his sav - ing grace; Let none whom

made all na - tions is not will - ing One soul should
stooped to save his lost cre - a - tion And died on
soul for them in prayer vic - to - rious, And haste the
he has ran - somed fail to greet him, Through your ne -

Refrain

per - ish, lost in shades of night.
earth that we might live a - bove.
com - ing of the glo - rious day. Pub - lish glad tid - ings, tid - ings of
glect, un - fit to see his face.

peace, Tid - ings of Je - sus, re - demp-tion, and re - lease.

Praise, My Soul, the King of Heaven

1 Praise, my soul, the King of heav - en; To his feet your trib - ute bring.
2 Praise him for his grace and fa - vor To our fore-bears in dis - tress.
3 Ten - der - ly he shields and spares us; Well our fee - ble frame he knows.
4 An - gels help us to a - dore him, Who be - hold him face to face.

Ran-somed, healed, re-stored, for - giv - en, Ev - er - more his prais - es sing.
Praise him, still the same for - ev - er, Slow to chide and swift to bless.
In his hands he gent - ly bears us, Res - cues us from all our foes.
Sun and moon bow down be - fore him; All who dwell in time and space.

Al - le - lu - ia! Al - le - lu - ia! Praise the ev - er - last - ing King!
Al - le - lu - ia! Al - le - lu - ia! Glo - rious in his faith - ful - ness!
Al - le - lu - ia! Al - le - lu - ia! Wide - ly as his mer - cy flows.
Al - le - lu - ia! Al - le - lu - ia! Praise with us the God of grace.

What a Friend We Have in Jesus

1 What a friend we have in Je - sus, All   our sins and griefs to   bear!
2 Have we tri - als and temp - ta - tions? Is   there trou-ble an - y - where?
3 Are we weak and heav - y - lad - en, Cum-bered with a load of   care?

What a priv - i - lege to car - ry Ev - 'ry-thing to God in   prayer!
We should nev - er be dis - cour-aged— Take   it   to the Lord in   prayer.
Pre - cious Sav - ior, still our ref - uge— Take   it   to the Lord in   prayer.

Oh, what peace we of - ten for - feit; Oh,   what need-less pain we bear—
Can we   find a friend so faith - ful Who   will   all our sor - rows share?
Do your friends de-spise, for - sake you? Take   it   to the Lord in   prayer.

All be-cause we do not car - ry Ev - 'ry-thing to God in   prayer!
Je - sus knows our ev - 'ry weak-ness— Take   it   to the Lord in   prayer.
In   his arms he'll take and shield you; You   will find a   so - lace there.

Index of Hymns

Bibliography

Ambrose

The Proper for the Lesser Feasts and Fasts. New York: The Church Hymnal Corporation, 1980.

Von Campenhausen, Hans. *The Fathers of the Latin Church.* Translated by Manfred Hoffman. London: Adam & Charles Black, 1964.

Athanasius

Farmer, David Hugh. *The Oxford Dictionary of Saints.* Oxford: Oxford University Press, 1978.

The Proper for the Lesser Feasts and Fasts. New York: The Church Hymnal Corporation, 1980.

Von Campenhausen, Hans. *The Fathers of the Greek Church.* Translated by Stanley Godman. New York: Pantheon Books, Inc., 1959.

Augustine of Hippo

Farmer, David Hugh. *The Oxford Dictionary of Saints.* Oxford: Oxford University Press, 1978.

The Proper for the Lesser Feasts and Fasts. New York: The Church Hymnal Corporation, 1980.

Von Campenhausen, Hans. *The Fathers of the Latin Church.* Translated by Manfred Hoffman. London: Adam & Charles Black, 1964.

Calvin, John

Noll, Mark A. 1994. "John Calvin." *Academic American Encyclopedia.* Grolier Electronic Publishing, Inc. PRODIGY.

Carey, William

Miller, Basil. *William Carey: The Father of Modern Missions.* Minneapolis: Bethany House Publishers, 1980.

Tucker, Ruth A. *From Jerusalem to Irian Jaya.* Grand Rapids: Zondervan, 1983.

Carmichael, Amy

Elliot, Elisabeth. *A Chance to Die: The Life and Legacy of Amy Carmichael*. Old Tappan, N.J.: Fleming H. Revell Company, 1987.

Tucker, Ruth A. *From Jerusalem to Irian Jaya*. Grand Rapids: Zondervan, 1983.

Chrysostom, John

Farmer, David Hugh. *The Oxford Dictionary of Saints*. Oxford: Oxford University Press, 1978.

The Proper for the Lesser Feasts and Fasts. New York: The Church Hymnal Corporation, 1980.

Von Campenhausen, Hans. *The Fathers of the Greek Church*. Translated by Stanley Godman. New York: Pantheon Books, Inc., 1959.

Elliot, Jim and the Auca martyrs

Elliot, Elisabeth. *Shadow of the Almighty*. New York: Harper Brothers, 1958.

Tucker, Ruth A. *From Jerusalem to Irian Jaya*. Grand Rapids: Zondervan, 1983.

Knox, John

Noll, Mark A. 1994. "John Knox." *Academic American Encyclopedia*. Grolier Electronic Publishing, Inc. PRODIGY.

Luther, Martin

Booth, Edwin P. *Martin Luther*. Westwood, N.J.: Barbour & Company, Inc., 1988.

Spitz, Lewis W. 1994. "Martin Luther." *Academic American Encyclopedia*. Grolier Electronic Publishing, Inc. PRODIGY.

Moon, Lottie

Tucker, Ruth A. *From Jerusalem to Irian Jaya*. Grand Rapids: Zondervan, 1983.

Mother Teresa

Doig, Desmond. *Mother Teresa: Her People and Her Work*. New York: Harper & Row, 1976.

Muggeridge, Malcolm. *Something Beautiful for God: Mother Teresa of Calcutta*. Garden City, N.Y.: Doubleday & Co., Inc., 1977.

Perpetua

Farmer, David Hugh. *The Oxford Dictionary of Saints*. Oxford: Oxford University Press, 1978.

The Proper for the Lesser Feasts and Fasts. New York: The Church Hymnal
Corporation, 1980.

Polycarp

Farmer, David Hugh. *The Oxford Dictionary of Saints.* Oxford: Oxford University
Press, 1984.
The Proper for the Lesser Feasts and Fasts. New York: The Church Hymnal
Corporation, 1980.

Taylor, Hudson

Tucker, Ruth A. *From Jerusalem to Irian Jaya.* Grand Rapids: Zondervan, 1983.

Townsend, William Cameron

Tucker, Ruth A. *From Jerusalem to Irian Jaya.* Grand Rapids: Zondervan, 1983.

Wesley, Charles and John

Ayling, Stanley. *John Wesley.* Nashville: Abingdon Press, 1979.
The Proper for the Lesser Feasts and Fasts. New York: The Church Hymnal
Corporation, 1980.

Other Sources

Connelly, J. "All Saints." *New Westminster Dictionary of Liturgy and Worship.* Edited
by J. G. Davies. Philadelphia: Westminster Press, 1986.
Cowie, L. W. and John Selwyn Gummer. *The Christian Calendar.* Springfield: G. &
C. Merriam Company, 1974.
Lang, Jovian P. *Dictionary of Liturgy.* New York: Catholic Book Publishing
Company, 1989.
Smalley, Stephen S. "All Saints' Day." *New International Dictionary of the Christian
Church.* Edited by J. D. Douglas. Grand Rapids: Zondervan, 1974.
Smith, C. "All Saints' Day." *New Catholic Dictionary.* Edited by William J.
McDonald. Washington, D.C.: Catholic University Press, 1967.
Zimmerman, Martha. *Celebrating the Christian Year.* Minneapolis: Bethany House
Publishers, 1993.

FAMILY CELEBRATIONS AT THANKSGIVING

And Alternatives to Halloween

Also by Ann Hibbard
Family Celebrations at Easter
Family Celebrations at Christmas